THE LAND OF
THE RED
DRAGON

CARDIFF

UNIVERSITY OF WALES PRESS

PUBLISHED JOINTLY BY

THE GIRL GUIDES ASSOCIATION OF WALES

AND

THE UNIVERSITY OF WALES PRESS BOARD

ⓒ 1979

COPYRIGHT FOR ALL COUNTRIES. ALL RIGHTS RESERVED

For sale in U.K. only

First edition as *The Welsh Gift Book*	1950
Second edition revised *The Land of the Red Dragon*	1953
Second impression	1957
Third edition revised	1969, 1972
Fourth edition	1979

ISBN 0 7083 0716 7

ACKNOWLEDGEMENTS

The compilers and publishers of this book wish to acknowledge their indebtedness to those who hold the copyright of the illustrations of the *Welsh Gift Book*.

Messrs. John Miller, Ltd., for illustrations from *The Bangor Guide*.

The British Publishing Co., Ltd., for illustrations from their publication *Pembrokeshire* by Miss M. Wight.

Messrs. B. T. Batsford, Ltd., and The Central Office of Information for the photograph of *The Rhondda Valley*.

Messrs. E. D. J. Burrow & Co., Ltd., for illustrations from *The Montgomeryshire County Hand Book*.

The National Museum of Wales for illustrations.

Mr. K. E. Neill and The Colwyn Bay Corporation for considerable help and advice over illustrations.

The Gower Society for the photograph of *Gower*.

The Dominion Press for the photograph of *The Welsh Dancers*.

Mr. Norman Tucker for the photograph of *The Church of St. Celynin* and The Girl Guide Association for the loan of line blocks.

Dr. Iorwerth Peate and The Brython Press for illustrations.

The British Broadcasting Corporation for illustrations.

The Ministry of Public Building and Works for a photograph of *Caernarvon Castle*.

The Director of Education of Montgomeryshire and the Education Committee for help and illustrations.

The Montgomeryshire Express for help with illustrations.

Urdd Gobaith Cymru for help with illustrations.

Thanks are also due to the photographers whose work is reproduced in these pages, among them: Mr. H. A. Coulter, Miss M. Wight, Mr. J. Dixon-Scott, Mr. W. W. Harris, Mr. E. J. Brown, Mr. Evan Evans, Mr. R. C. Hughes, Mr. K. E. Neill, Mr. J. D. K. Lloyd and Mrs. E. Pettitt, Mr. Harold Morris, Miss Sylvia Lewes, Miss Dilys McWhan, Mr. E. Owen Jones, Mr. Llywelyn Williams, Mr. Llew. Morgan, Mr. F. Leonard Jackson, Mrs. B. M. Pursell and Mr. Justin B. Ingram.

FOREWORD

THERE are many to thank for bringing this book into being, and we owe much to distinguished people who have encouraged, helped, and advised us. Some have written for us or lent us their works; others have given most generous permission to use special matter, illustrations and music, of which they hold the copyright.

We are deeply grateful to Professor E. G. Bowen, Dr. Iorwerth C. Peate, Cynan (Dr. A. E. Jones), Professor and Mrs. Thomas Jones, Miss Cassie Davies, Dr. North, Miss Eiluned Lewis, Miss Melfin Jones, Mrs. Lois Blake, Mr. Glyn Davies, Mr. D. C. Owen, Mr. Gwilym Williams, Mr. J. A. Davies, and to the many others who have so readily helped us. In addition we wish to thank the National Museum of Wales for their generous assistance, and Dr. Elwyn Davies for valuable advice and for the unfailing interest and care which he has taken over the publication of THE LAND OF THE RED DRAGON in 1953 and the second impression in 1957; also to Dr. R. Brinley Jones for ably carrying forward this work with the new 1969 edition.

For permission to use copyright matter we are indebted to the following: Messrs. Hughes a'i Fab for extracts from *The Hour Glass* and *Welsh Folk Songs*, Messrs. Staples Press, Ltd., for extracts from *These Things Remain*, Messrs. Lovat Dixon and Thompson, Ltd., Messrs. Peter Davies, Ltd., for *The Birthright*, Messrs. Harper and Brothers for an extract from *Facing the Stars*, Messrs. J. M. Dent and the Trustees for the copyrights of the late Dylan Thomas for an extract from '*A Winter's Tale*' by Dylan Thomas, Messrs. Jonathan Cape and Mrs. H. M. Davies for '*That Golden Time*' by W. H. Davies, and Miss Nancy Thomas for '*The Stones of St. David's*'.

Last, but not least, we would like to say 'Thank you' for the interest shown in our attempt to bring into being a book in which we have tried to set out the story of Wales, with its history and ancient traditions forming a background for young people on whom the future of Wales depends.

This book, which is issued by the Girl Guide Association of Wales, was originally produced under the title of THE WELSH GIFT BOOK. This was followed by an enlarged edition under the new title of THE LAND OF THE RED DRAGON. Later a second impression of the book was issued together with a special abridged edition for schools. We were grateful for the help and guidance given by the Publication Advisory Panel of the Welsh Joint Education Committee in the preparation of this Schools edition.

I originally compiled this book to further the knowledge of the Guides of Wales in the background of their own land and with the hope that it would travel to many countries all over the world where there are Guides. This has not only come true but repeated requests have been received from outside the Guide Movement for a wider circulation. For this reason under their present Chief Commissioner —The Hon. Gwenllian Philipps, who has taken a keen interest in the book since its inception—the Executive Committee of the Welsh Guide Council have agreed to go forward with a further revised and enlarged edition of THE LAND OF THE RED DRAGON.

In the third edition I widened the scope of the book to make it of equal value to young or older people who are interested in Wales; and the opportunity has been taken in this fourth edition to make some small changes which bring it further up to date. It is our hope that the book may take with it a message of friendship and something of the spirit of Wales to those who may know little of our country.

In every land traditions lie deep in the hearts of the people; in folk-life, in song, in music, in craft, in language, in drama, and in legends. There are rites and customs that are precious and link us all through love of our Country, not only here in Wales but far overseas.

Olwin Kay

Chief Commissioner for Wales 1944/54
Girl Guide Association

SCOTS PINE

CONTENTS

WELSH MUSIC

NATIONAL FOLK SONGS

Wele Gwawriodd—Lo! A Day Dawned

Bugeilio'r Gwenith Gwyn—Watching the Wren

Suo Gan—Lullaby

Robin Goch—Robin Redbreast

Dechreuad y Byd—The Beginning of the World

Ar Hyd y Nos—All Through the Night

Dafydd y Garreg Wen—David of the White Rock

Cyfri'r Geifr—Counting the Goats

LLANWDDYN JIG

Croen y Ddafad Felan—The Yellow Sheepskin

WALES
HER PEOPLE, THEIR COUNTRY
AND CULTURE

The hills will be here after us,
The silent strength that lent us aid;
The little shrines of words or deeds
On ways our fathers made.

MELFIN JONES

The Birthright

We who were born
In country places,
Far from cities
And shifting faces,
We have a birthright
No man can sell,
And a secret joy
No man can tell.

For we are kindred
To lordly things:
The wild duck's flight
And the white owl's wings
To pike and salmon,
To bull and horse,
The curlew's cry
And the smell of the gorse.

Pride of trees,
Swiftness of streams,
Magic of frost
Have shaped our dreams.
No baser vision
Their spirit fills
Who walk by right
On the naked hills.

EILUNED LEWIS

CARN INGLI AND PENTRE IFAN CROMLECH

M. Wight

E. G. BOWEN

An Introduction to Wales

WALES, it is said, is a western peninsula of England and, indeed, if you look at a map of the British Isles you will find that this is perfectly true. If, on the other hand, you visit Wales and walk over its hills and through its valleys and talk to the people you will soon discover that there is more to it than that. You will find yourself in a separate country where the people speak a different language and think in a different way from the people of England. You will soon be convinced that it is not a peninsula of England at all. Take one more look at the maps and you will find that the western fringe of the European continent has many other peninsulas and islands reaching out to the Atlantic. There is Brittany, Cornwall, Ireland, the Isle of Man, the Galloway peninsula, the Hebrides, and hosts of peninsulas and islands off western Scotland, which, like Wales, have an independent life of their own. Their distinctiveness has, however, a common basis in that they share an inheritance of Celtic speech. Some 2,000 years ago the peoples of all these lands spoke some dialect of Celtic speech, and the ease with which people travelled from one peninsula to another and from one island to the other in early times gave these Celtic lands not only a common language but also a common culture. It is true that in modern times far fewer people speak the Celtic languages in these parts of Europe than was formerly the case, but in Wales Celtic speech has survived in modern times to a much greater extent than it has in Ireland, Scotland and the Isle of Man. At present about 542,000 people, some 20 per cent of the population, are able to speak Welsh. No one can hope to understand Wales who does not realize that it is, and has been for long ages past, a part of the Celtic Fringe of Europe and through its language and culture it has more in common with Ireland or Brittany than it has with England.

If we now take a closer look at the map of Wales we see at a glance that it is a land of hills and valleys. There is a great mass of highlands stretching down the country like the back of a tortoise. In the north-west, around Snowdon, it is very high and here we have real mountain country with steep slopes, bare of soil, and deep dark valleys filled with beautiful long lakes. This land is the delight of the tourist and holiday maker. We can follow the highland southwards through the Harlech and Berwyn mountains, past Cader Idris to the moorlands of Plinlimon in central Wales. Without a break the high ground passes south-eastwards to merge into the Brecon Beacons. The moorlands of the south and centre are different from the mountains of the north-west in so far as they are more rounded in form and are grass covered and, therefore, not quite so attractive to the eye. From this great central upland, valleys radiate in all directions. The Conway and the Clwyd and many more to the northern plain; the Dyfi, the Ystwyth, and the Teifi, and their companions to the westward; the Cleddau, the Towy, the Nedd, and the Afan southward; and even longer and more important rivers flow eastward like the Dee, the Severn, the Usk, and the Wye. This all-important picture will help you to understand a great deal about Wales.

To begin with, this highland core lies in the path of the Atlantic gales, and the amount of rain that falls on upland Wales during the year is very considerable. The land is rain-swept and wind-swept, wet underfoot, and the soils are poor. In consequence the grasses that are able to grow there are also poor and, except in summer time, unsatisfying for sheep and cattle. The valleys and the lower lands are a little

I

more favoured in this respect but they, too, receive much rainfall and have little sunshine and are more suited for pastoral farming than for the growing of crops. So it is that the Welsh farmer has throughout the ages been a pastoralist, relying on his sheep and cattle rather than on his ploughed fields. He has placed his homestead either on the lower valley slopes or on the valley bottoms, and in the old days he would follow his flocks and herds up to the high grazings in summer and return again to the lower land in winter. The picture we have of Welsh tribal society in the Middle Ages is typical of pastoral societies found elsewhere in the world. The people were organized into tribal groups which were knit together by the fact that all the male members claimed descent from a common ancestor. Blood relationship was very important, as social status depended upon it. The individual was a member of a vast family that went far beyond his immediate parents, grandparents, brothers, and sisters. Much of this survives in an unseen way into modern life, and all who know Wales well know how important it is to understand this aspect of things at the present time.

If we think again of the central core of moorland and the radiating valleys on all sides, we see the origin of some other aspects of Welsh life. The little country has no convenient centre—the real centre would be on the top of these moorlands in central Wales. No one, however, lives there and no capital could ever grow up in this position. Instead Welsh people have tended to live in separate groups centred in these many valleys. One aspect of this lack of a capital city until modern times is the fact that the great national institutions of Wales move round from year to year, visiting towns large and small in turn. In this way the National Eisteddfod functions. This institution is a great competitive meeting where choirs, musicians and poets compete with one another for prizes. One year the festival may be held in Cardiff, the next year in Caernarfon and the year after it will move somewhere else. The Welsh people love singing and great hymn singing festivals (Cymanfa Ganu) are another feature of the life of the country. Now one local centre holds

FOEL GOCH

H. A. Coulter

2

VYRNWY RIVER

J. D. K. Lloyd

its meeting, now another. Now the singers gather at this chapel, now at that one. Likewise the governing bodies of the various churches in Wales go around from one place to another for their meeting from year to year; so does the Archbishopric of the Church in Wales migrate as a new Archbishop is elected. Every place must get its turn and so even the national institutions are broken into small pieces so that each area should have something. The University of Wales is not at one place, but in a number of widely scattered Colleges and Institutes. Similarly, while the National Museum of Wales is at Cardiff, the National Library is at Aberystwyth. It is no wonder, therefore, that in recent times, when every effort was made to find a capital for Wales, almost every town wished to stake its claim. The controversy ended at last in 1955 when Cardiff, the largest and most important city, was officially designated capital, although this modern city is completely cut off from the traditions of the Welsh-speaking farmers of the hills. Nevertheless, these radiating valleys all look outward from Wales either to the sea or eastwards towards England. This has had some interesting effects. Into the eastward-facing valleys and along the coastal plains English speech and English ways of life have spread throughout the ages, so that the eastern borderland, particularly in Montgomeryshire, Radnorshire, and Breconshire, is now English in speech and so is much of the north Wales coast as far as Bangor and in the south the Vale of Glamorgan, Gower, and south Pembrokeshire. On the other hand the outward-looking valleys have helped many a Welshman either to migrate to new lands overseas, or, more frequently, to migrate to England to seek his fortunes anew. The effect of these movements has been to deprive the countryside of some of its better elements. Yet, as the Welsh people became outward rather than inward looking, they developed an interest in others; they have always welcomed strangers gladly and are famous for their hospitality. What is even more important is that they have developed an interest in other people and in their ways of life, and so Wales has played a prominent part in all movements for world peace and understanding among the nations.

Such would have been a reasonably complete picture of Wales and its people were it not for the fact that both in the north and in the south of the country there are important coal-fields. The south Wales

3

coal-field is one of the largest and most important in the British Isles while the one in Flintshire and Denbighshire is somewhat smaller. These coal-fields have been developed during the last 150 years and they have attracted many families from the Welsh hills to come and live in these parts, thereby further increasing the drainage of population from the countryside. At first only the menfolk came to the industrial regions to work—returning to their farms at harvest time and at other important seasons of the year. When, however, the railways became established in the middle of the nineteenth century, people came to live permanently on the coal-fields and (what was more important) people came to live in south Wales from all over the British Isles as well as from other parts of Wales. This meant that the Welsh culture brought from the hills became diluted and the English language the only language understood by all the workmen from different parts of the British Isles. At present we have, therefore, more than half the population of Wales living within a radius of thirty miles of the city of Cardiff, and their cultural life is neither wholly English nor wholly Welsh.

Another important factor affected the fortunes of the south Wales coal-field. The excellent quality of the coal and the ease with which it could be exported down the seaward-running valleys to the great ports of Cardiff, Barry, Newport, Port Talbot, and Swansea meant that few industries based on coal developed in south Wales itself and full reliance was placed on export. In this way far more people outside Wales knew about Welsh coal than knew about Welsh people. All went well until the world demand for Welsh coal changed after the First World War. Then disaster followed. Unemployment became rife and reached serious proportions, and migration of young Welsh industrial workers to the newer industries in England started a new phase in the general Welsh exodus. In the years between the Great Wars the government did what it could to establish light industries in these depressed areas, but many economic and social problems are still unsolved.

North-western Wales—the old territory of Gwynedd—is still the most Welsh in character. Throughout most of its area over 80 per cent of the people can speak Welsh. The unit of settlement in the upland and mountain land is the traditional single farm with the isolated nonconformist chapel often the only local focus of social life. In recent years great changes have taken place. Many of the farms have become non-viable economic units and amalgamation of holdings has been marked by the consequent depopulation. Furthermore the towns, which are far more anglicized than their hinterland, help to denude the countryside by a process of in-migration, allowing the empty farms and cottages to be bought by newcomers largely from the English cities. In this way many farms are reconditioned and used as places for retirement or as second homes. Meanwhile the immediate coastal zone has seen the full development of the tourist industry. Social patterns in consequence have greatly changed even in this, possibly the most characteristically Welsh area in the whole of Wales.

Three things lovable in man; peace, wisdom, and kindness.

Three things for which thanks are due; an invitation, a gift, and a warning.

Three things which bring a man the love of neighbours; to be a peacemaker, to be a helper,

and to be a guide.

Three ways to know a man; by his discourse, his conduct, and his companions.

Three things which the miser obtains through his wealth; pain gathering,

care in keeping, and fear of losing.

(TRIADS FROM THE BLACK BOOK OF CARMARTHEN, 12TH CENT.)

PETER LEWIS

Religious and Historical Background

WELSH history is very ancient and very simple, so historically it is but a stone's throw to return to the pages of the *Itinerary through Wales* written in 1188 by Giraldus. He was engaged at the time on a recruiting campaign—for the Third Crusade, when he was accompanied appropriately by an Archbishop, though an Englishman. The Welsh, he records, are of sharp and acute intellect, gifted with a rich and powerful understanding, proud of their lineage, fond of conversation, uttering their jokes in a light and easy manner; yet they are no less light in mind than in body, they are quarrelsome and warlike, 'ready after defeat to return immediately to action'.

Now Gerald was born at Manorbier in Pembrokeshire. His grandmother was the spirited princess Nest, the 'Helen of Wales', mistress of Henry the First. In his early days he indulged the Welsh passion for tribal warfare, returning from a lecture tour in Paris to secure, as an archdeacon of Brecon, the excommunication of the Bishop of St. Asaph for trespassing on the rights of St. David's. Later, however, after a distinguished career as politician, ecclesiastic, and author, he became champion of Welsh rights, and made it his ambition to elevate St. David's to the status of a Metropolitan See deriving authority direct from Rome—always with the proviso that he was himself to be the Bishop. Henry II turned him down for the bishopric because he was a Welshman of royal blood, but nothing daunted Gerald repaired to Rome, where he greatly entertained the Pope with his amusing stories, though he failed entirely to secure his ends.

A renewed desire for independence is alive in many hearts in Wales today; to understand how this has developed it is well to go back and seek some of the origins of Welsh feelings and behaviour.

First in importance comes the geographical situation described by Professor Bowen in his Introduction. Wales is a mountain fringe on the great continent of Europe. Thus the movements of mankind westward across the plains have broken at last like waves against the flanks of our hills, leaving in the valleys and on the habitable slopes the traces of each succeeding tide. Wales as the ultimate barrier stores the secrets of the past, long since drowned and lost along the lowland flats.

But also there has always been the great back-doorway of the sea, sheltered by Ireland from the worst Atlantic gales, providing in the sweep of Cardigan Bay, in the inlets of the south and the promontories of the north, shores where settlers and traders from the Mediterranean have found welcome landfall and a lasting home. So the Welsh not only look out from their grazing grounds across England's coloured counties; the sons of farmers and fishermen have also followed the sea from one generation to another.

Indeed the earliest known influences in Wales were sea-borne. The cromlechs, rock linings of vanished earthen mounds, are recognized as the remains of the 'pyramids of Wales'. They were built as tombs by a people believed to be non-Aryan, who came by sea from Spain and the Mediterranean, some 2,000 years before Christ. The number of their megaliths about the coasts of Wales proves the long ages that these folk inhabited our shores. How far the traces of this pre-Celtic people persist in the

ST. DAVID'S CATHEDRAL

M. Wight

The Stones of St. David's

We can remember the throes of creation,
Terrible years of pressure and pain,
Till, purged of all weakness, we found our vocation
Guarding the land from the storms and the rain.
Purple and green through the waves and the rain.

Centuries past, and the sea-birds came wheeling,
Wildflowers sprang through the quickening sod.
All nature rejoiced and its secret revealing
We knew we were made for the glory of God,
Beauty and strength for the glory of God.

Centuries past, and the first men came, slowly
Raising stone circles with primitive skill.
They knew, as we know that the headland was holy.
We waited in patience to serve the Lord's will.
We had been destined to serve the Lord's will.

Then came the hour of our blessed consummation
We were riven and tamed, diminished and torn,
From the birds and the sea for the wondrous creation
To the glory of God when the great Church was born
We had come home when the great Church was born.

Oh, worshippers kneel on us, handle us, love us,
We may still feel regrets for the old pagan days,
For the sound of the waves and the seagulls above us,
Remember it all in your prayers and your praise.
All time and all space in one paean of praise.

NANCY THOMAS

6

country today it is impossible to judge; but Professor Zimmern once remarked: 'To watch a Welsh audience sitting spell-bound, sometimes for hours, under the sway of a call to the unknown, is to be transported from the little corner in Western Europe in which a sport of fate has set this peculiar people to the vast plains and deserts of Asia.'

Moving from the Stone Age to the borders of history the language of Wales is the speech of the Brythonic Celts, who arrived in Britain some 400 years before Christ. Certainly fair-haired Celtic types can be seen in the country today; more remarkable is the fact, established in the Census of 1931, that nearly one million of the total population of two and a half million in that year were Welsh-speaking men and women. In the counties of Anglesey, Caernarfon, Merioneth, Cardigan, and Carmarthen the proportion was over 700 per 1,000 inhabitants. These are striking figures in a tiny country exposed for 2,000 years to all the influence of a border state.

The Welsh way of life can be seen to have baffled invaders. Like the children of Israel, the Welsh were a tribal race. Because they kept flocks and herds, moving from summer pasture to valley home-stead, a family was known, not by its habitation, but by its lineage. Thus loss of a piece of disputed land by no means spelt defeat for its former possessor.

As a pastoral people, moreover, the Welsh did not live in villages, and did not for long centuries gather together into towns. They lived, as they do today, scattered about the ground they had won from forest, marsh, and barren hill. There were no cities for marauders to burn, nor citadels for men-at-arms to demolish; invaders retreated in despair finding nothing worthy of reduction, often to be ambushed and slaughtered at the gorge or ford. Angry Powers in England were forced to build elabo-rate castles round the outposts of the hills and coasts, but the Welsh had no occasion to submit until they chose to do so, when their own Tudor family were established on the throne next door.

But although the Welsh tribes were impossible to catch and overcome, they were continually divided among themselves. In the days of King Arthur, the Christian kingdom of the west included Cornwall and Cumberland; but even when Wales came to be contained by Offa's Dyke it was only on a few occasions and under exceptional princes that the feuds of north and south were quelled, to present a united front against outside opponents. 'That great magician, damn'd Glendower' almost alone stands out, his meteoric career blazing like the comet which appeared in the heavens high above Glyn Dyfrdwy in the spring of 1402. Owen Glendower (Glyndŵr) by his struggle against Henry IV won recognition for Wales from Scotland, Ireland, and France, and held parliaments of the nation at Machynlleth and at Harlech, the former being traditionally associated with the crowning of Owen as Prince of Wales in the presence of envoys from Scotland, Spain, France, and every commote of the country. But though he drove the English in fear into their walled towns and castles, though he welcomed in 1405 a large French force at Milford Haven, and with them moved into England as far as Woodbury Hill, near Worcester, his cause at length declined, his dreams and hopes dispersed. In 1410 he vanished, his resting-place unknown, but his fame for ever bright.

With the Tudors enthroned in London modern Welsh history begins. Socially Wales had 'arrived'; in English literature the Cambrian came into fashion. References scattered through Shakespeare show that in his day it was still popular to mention the valour of the Welsh troops at Agincourt and Bosworth, and to refer to Elizabeth's kingly ancestor as 'Harry of Monmouth'. Wales enjoyed an esteem among English writers which was not repeated until the golden age of Wordsworth, Southey, Coleridge, and Hazlitt, who came to discover afresh the 'wildwood scenery and terrible grace' of the mountains beyond Severn, Dee, and Wye.

THE CHURCH OF ST. CELYNIN, LLANGELYNIN

The church stands 1,000 feet above sea-level, among remains of prehistoric and early medieval settlements. A holy well in a corner of the burial ground indicates that the foundation dates back to the early days of Welsh Christianity.

In the Beginning was the Word

GUIDANCE: For Thou wilt light my candle, the Lord God will enlighten my darkness.

PROMISE: No man having set his hand to the plough and looking back is fit for the Kingdom of God.

LAW: The law of the Lord is an undefiled law. . . .

COURAGE: Be thou strong and very courageous . . . and the Lord thy God goeth with thee whithersoever thou goest.

FREEDOM: And ye shall know the truth and the truth shall make you free.

FRIENDSHIP: By love serve one another.

SERVICE: Inasmuch as ye have done it unto one of these the least of my brethren, ye have done it unto me.

INTEGRITY: I will lift up mine eyes unto the hills from whence cometh my help; my help cometh from the Lord who has made heaven and earth; He will not suffer thy foot to be moved.

HAPPINESS: Let all those who put their trust in Thee rejoice.

PEACE: In calmness and in confidence shall be your strength.

IORWERTH C. PEATE

Welsh Life since 1536

THE year 1536 marked the beginning of a new era in the history of Wales. In that year 'An Act for Laws and Justice to be ministered in Wales in like form as it is in this Realm' (27 Henry VIII, c. 26) was passed; it 'ordained enacted and established' that Wales should be 'incorporated, united and annexed' to England. In itself this Act of Union epitomizes a number of laws enacted between 1535 and 1543 which decreed the abolition of the Marcher Lordships as political units, the division of the Marches into shires, the abolition of the Courts of the Lordships, the creation of the Courts of Great Sessions, the provision of members of Parliament for Welsh shires and boroughs, the abolition of the remaining Welsh laws and of Welsh custom and the outlawing of the Welsh language, 'a speech nothing like, nor consonant to the natural Mother Tongue used within this Realm'. Consequently 'no Person or Persons that use the Welsh Speech or Language shall have or enjoy any Manner, Office or Fees within this Realm of England, Wales or other the King's Dominion, upon pain of forfeiting the same Offices or Fees, unless he or they use and exercise the English Speech or Language'. It may be remembered in passing that though this last section of the Act has never been rigorously enforced it still remains on the Statute Book.

The Tudors were a family of Welsh descent and their accession to the English throne was therefore a matter of profound significance in the history of Wales. Briefly stated, it formed a belief in Wales in the creation of a Welsh hegemony which would wipe out the disastrous consequences of the partial conquest of the country in 1282. The accession of the great-grandson of a cousin of Owain Glyndŵr, Maredudd, who had been hanged, drawn, and quartered for his help in the fight for Welsh independence in the beginning of the fifteenth century could hardly be looked upon by Welsh people in any other light. But the times had changed and the Tudors, in the age of the absolutism of 'the new monarchy', cared only for consolidating their kingdom at the expense of their native country and language, even though Henry Tudor had gained Welsh support by an appeal to a sense of nationalism and was himself, of course, Welsh speaking. The tragedy lay in the fact that the Welsh nobles trusted too completely in the Tudor monarchs.

Henry VII laid the foundation for this trust by repealing the many harsh laws enacted for Wales in previous years, by giving his heir a Welsh name and by rewarding lavishly the Welsh nobles who had helped to secure him the English throne. The consequences were manifold.

Wales, between 1282 and 1536, was not a completely conquered country. An upland country on the western fringe of the English plain, it had been subjected only partially to the indignity of conquest, the social effects of which were few. The shires sent no representatives to the English Parliament and the English boroughs were 'little more than islands in a Welsh sea'. The Welsh system of gavelkind was not abolished and the Welsh language and its literature suffered no setback. Indeed 'it is a well-known fact that Welsh thought and Welsh social life during that period were in greater harmony with European thought and life than they have ever been since'. It was in many respects the Golden Age of Welsh literature and of Welsh social life. 'The vigorous and splendid social life mirrored in countless poems— the chieftains whose tables were loaded with the choicest of foreign fruits, currants, cinnamon and oranges from the south, and the wines of Rochelle, Bordeaux, and Gascony, whose walls were hung with the rich tapestry of Arras, and whose dwellings resounded with the music of harps; the splendour of the monasteries, the "gold adorned choir", the crystal windows, the lofty roofs resplendent with the bearings of princes, the light of torches and the burning of incense, the rich tombs with sculptured figures and arms of the dead,—this is not the reflection of a rude and barbaric society'. In this society cultural activity reached a very high standard. Each nobleman had his bard and 'in no period of Welsh history was there so prolific, so scholarly, or so finished an output. It contrasted strangely with the condition of contemporary literature in England where a deep silence had fallen on the land.' Mansion and monastery were the centres of a cultural life of a high order. But the year 1536 sounded its death-knell.

The legislation represented by the Act of Union made Wales politically a province of England. It shattered the social system by its insistence upon the right of primogeniture; it attempted to wreck Welsh culture by placing a taboo upon the language of nobleman, bard, and peasant; moreover it tore at the roots of the Welsh literary tradition by classifying the itinerant bards as 'vagrants'. It caused the loyal nobility to turn to the English court where they became office-holders and familiar figures, as Tudor literature testifies. Furthermore the Tudors 'created a new nobility from the [increasing middle-class]; these were given offices, the lands taken from the monasteries were apportioned between them . . . they were bribed to loyalty and transformed into Englishmen'. And while the bards continued to find patrons in Wales in the sixteenth century, it must be stressed that they became steadily fewer as the landed class became increasingly anglicized.

But the year 1536 marked the end of the old order in still another direction. In that year the monasteries which had been, despite much justifiable criticism of them, the centres of native culture, were suppressed and their lands acquired by the smaller gentry. This disappearance of the monastic establishments had a profound effect upon human development. At one blow, the peasantry were deprived not only of their spiritual advisers but of their patrons in agriculture, craftsmanship, and literature. Few aspects of Tudor policy in Wales had a more devastating effect.

This then was the condition of Wales at the Reformation. On the one hand, its old nobility (with some notable exceptions) and its smaller gentry secure in their belief in a Welsh 'victory' aped their leaders by becoming more English than the English themselves. They adopted the English language, English dress, introduced English architecture into their Welsh homes, adopted English furniture (the two-tier cupboard was soon to become known as the *cwpwrdd deuddarn* and *tridarn* and the 'Welsh dresser' to assume especial prominence). On the other hand the peasantry, orphaned of its patrons both civil and ecclesiastical, was left to its own devices. The Reformation, coming at this juncture, left the peasantry cold: for it was only an imposition by the English government. It was an imposition which was in many ways enforced with harshness and with corruption and though the peasantry accepted it without a struggle, it was still an unwilling acceptance by a people who clung to old loyalties and old customs.

Paradoxically as it may seem, it was the thoroughness of the Tudor attempt to anglicize Wales that caused its ultimate failure. John Penry (1559–93), the Puritan martyr, a native of the eastern fringe of the Welsh moorland, gives us a sad picture of the condition of the country in the early days of the re-formed church. Ultimately executed for his attacks on the Church, he had at an early stage in his short career pleaded for the translation of the Bible into Welsh. Elizabeth, in commanding its translation, stated expressly that its one aim was to aid the Welsh people to learn English. But in years to come it was the Welsh Bible in the hands of a literate peasant community that saved the Welsh language.

During this period of vain hope and bitter disillusion when the noblemen and the lesser gentry flocked to the English capital in the exultant belief expressed so deliberately by one of their foremost poets, Lewis Glyn Cothi: 'The Saxons' sway is over, it is high time for them to go into the wave before the firing of guns. No Saxon shall be seen free from tribute, nor Saxons any more in session, nor any

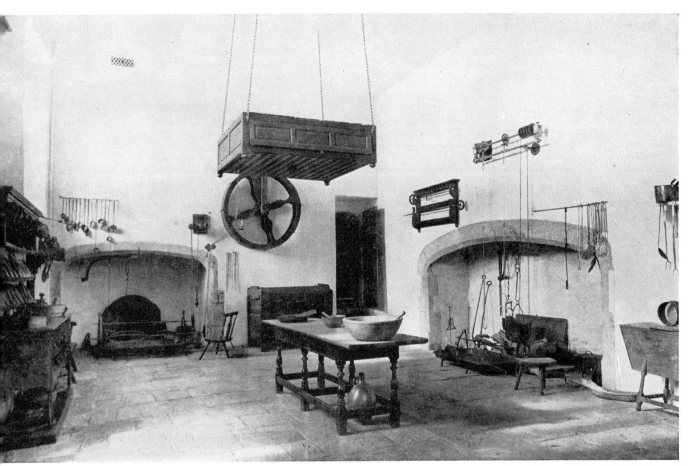

ELSH FOLK MUSEUM: THE KITCHEN — ST. FAGANS CASTLE   *The National Museum of Wales (Welsh Folk Museum)*

Saxon bearing office, not any couple of them but who are officeless'—during this period, life in Wales was to a high degree the life of a community depending upon farming, the raising of cattle and the rearing of sheep which gave rise to a flourishing trade in wool. This community had its crafts which in the few urban centres were organized into guilds. On the moorland, which forms the great core of Wales, the people lived in scattered homesteads which bore no resemblance to the rural communities of the English plain. Indeed, a survey of the moorland farmhouses leads one to note a closer affinity in house-types with the north of Britain and even with some of the ancient structures of parts of Scandinavia. Agriculture itself was primitive, and while it is true that some coal was mined and that lead was worked in, for instance, Montgomeryshire and Cardiganshire, the country showed no promise of any industrial expansion. The moorland—always the salvation of Wales—provided its wealth, and it is significant that the fall-line area of parts of Montgomeryshire, Radnorshire, and Brecknockshire provided for a long period not only the centres of a flourishing commerce but also of the patronage which made possible much of the literature of the period: one need only remind the reader of the associations of such a place as Hergest Court.

Finally, in dealing with the sixteenth century, mention should be made of the anglicized Welshmen. Some of these 'established the Tudor Grammar Schools in Wales, so that Welsh boys would be enabled to attain the same success in England as had fallen to their lot. With the Reformation the monastic schools and those of the chantry priests came to an end. Some of the revenues of the Church lands were allotted to the new schools, as, for example, to that of Abergavenny. The monastic school at Abergwili also was removed to Brecon, where it became Christ's College, the reason given . . . being that the people of Carmarthen knew no English. . . . Among [the schools were those] of Margam, Bangor, Presteign, Ruthin, Carmarthen, Caerleon and Cowbridge. They exercised a strong anglicizing influence.' In 1571 a Welsh college was established but it was decided to locate it at Oxford—Jesus College, founded by Dr. Hugh Price of Brecon. The culminating effect of Tudor policy in Wales therefore was to uproot its educated class from the old traditions, to turn its eyes towards the old English universities and to sow the seed of an idea, which while it appears in the sixteenth century in the bardic contention between William Cynwal of the native culture and Archdeacon Edmund Prys, a Cambridge graduate, was to flower in all its absurdity in the nineteenth century when scores of Welshmen believed that culture was synonymous with a knowledge of the English language and that only Oxford and Cambridge represented the ideal in culture and education.

The year 1536 was destined to have another direct influence of far-reaching importance upon the history of Wales. It was the year which saw the publication of John Calvin's *Institutes of the Christian Religion*: the Methodist Reformation (it is scarcely accurate to call it a Revival) of the eighteenth century was to make Calvin's outlook upon religion a Welsh way of life.

While we recall with gratitude the benefits bestowed upon Wales and upon her literature by a few outstanding figures of the Anglican clergy in the eighteenth century, such as Ellis Wynne, and Theophilus Evans, it is no exaggeration to say that the Established Church of that period was notable for its abuses and for its poverty. One should not forget, however, the work of the (Anglican) Society for the Promotion of Christian Knowledge with its excellent system of charity schools, its new edition of the Welsh Bible (although most of the teaching in the schools was in English) and its distribution of religious books and tracts. But the Society's schools were not, of course, the only schools then in existence in Wales. (The 'Old Nonconformists', whose story cannot be traced here, were also responsible for the establishment of scores of schools.) In the wake of the Society's diligent labours came Griffith Jones (1683–1761), rector of Llanddowror, Carmarthenshire, who may be considered the precursor of the Methodist movement. He set up a system of circulating schools, which at the time of his death had been responsible for teaching nearly 160,000 pupils. Although Jones's intention—he had been influenced by the Pietist Movement—was to save the souls of his countrymen, his great achievement was to save the life of the Welsh language. He taught the nation to read and imbued it with a sound knowledge of the magnificent language of the Welsh Bible. The work which he had thus initiated was expanded by the development of the Methodist movement whose apostle, Daniel Rowland, had been 'converted' by Jones's preaching. Howel Harris (1714–73), who was the moving spirit of this new Reformation, was a personal acquaintance of Griffith Jones; and William Williams (1716–91) of Pant-y-celyn, the Movement's hymn-writer and one of the greatest figures of Welsh literary history, was associated with him indirectly.

Calvin had laid down three important principles: the sovereignty of God, the total depravity of man, and the pre-ordained salvation of the elect. Theologically, these were the foundation stones of the Welsh movement of the eighteenth century. The great bulwark of the Methodist Movement, however, was the fact that it was founded upon the Welsh language itself, which now became a vehicle of expression for the *whole* life of the people in much the same way that it had been in the heyday of the Middle Ages: with the added importance that the peasant had now a means of basing his faith directly upon Calvinistic theology.

The influence of the Methodist movement on the Welsh nation was stupendous. It was natural that the older nonconformity, established since the seventeenth century, but making little headway in many districts, should gain experience from the new movement. In many directions the 'older' nonconformists were themselves Methodistized, and Independents and Baptists often became as methodist as the Calvinistic Methodists themselves. But the Unitarians and Quakers were little influenced. Apart from all other considerations, the Unitarians held to an 'extreme' doctrine; their leaders were keen

CARREG CENNEN CASTLE
J. D. K. Lloyd

MOELFRE — ANGLESEY
H. A. Coulter

BEAUMARIS CASTLE
H. A. Coulter

thinkers who were not to be led by mere oratory however sincere the orators might be. And so the Unitarians remained in possession of their Cardiganshire stronghold unable to make any headway in the moorland, founding new causes only in the populous centres, in the towns where the thinker was brought up against problems unknown to the peasant. The story of the Quakers is still more significant. A nest of folk in the Bala-Dolgelley district (which now became a stronghold of Methodism), a large number of them had emigrated to America in the last decade of the seventeenth century. Those that remained did not forgo their democratic principles of church government but leavened the Independent churches of the district which still bear to this day the signs of their influence. In other parts of the country, the Society of Friends refused to abandon its philosophy of church government for the allurement of numbers and gradually lost its hold upon a people for whom it had in different conditions many attractions.

Briefly stated, the Methodist movement changed the whole outlook and consequently the tone of the Welsh nation. The Welsh people became an earnestly religious and highly literate nation, devout, philosophical, and literary. The chapel with its various organized activities became the centre of its social and cultural life. The pastors became its leaders since its own gentry by the end of the eighteenth century had become completely anglicized in language and sentiment. Much of its folk-tradition—the folk dance, in particular—suffered in consequence but the loss of this aspect of peasant life was more than compensated by the cultural development of the mass of the peasantry. Towards the middle of the nineteenth century, the medieval *eisteddfod*—a court of the bards—was rehabilitated as a democratic competitive festival, national in its appeal, which stimulated a high percentage of the peasantry to interest themselves in the creative arts, in craftsmanship, and in research work of various kinds. The religious movement too initiated the production of books and periodicals from the large number of printing presses which were set up in the small country towns.

Indeed the eighteenth century witnessed a literary revival independent of the religious movement. Its opening years saw the production of *Y Bardd Cwsc*, the work of Ellis Wynne, undoubtedly one of the greatest masters of Welsh prose. Edward Lhuyd, the distinguished Welshman who was the Keeper of the Ashmolean Museum at Oxford, together with the Rev. Theophilus Evans, another prose-writer of great distinction, may be said to have provided an antiquarian basis for the subsequent literature of the century. Nor must the work of the Rev. Moses Williams, F.R.S., a native of Cardiganshire, in the collection and cataloguing of Welsh manuscripts be forgotten. Lewis Morris, a native of Anglesey, and his more attractive brothers, worked in the same direction, while another Anglesey poet, Goronwy Owen (1723–69), together with a few kindred spirits, resuscitated the old bardic metres and founded a 'school of Welsh Augustans'. London Welshmen, actuated by antiquarian motives, founded patriotic societies such as the Honourable Society of Cymmrodorion (1751) which helped to promote the study of the antiquities, literature, and language of Wales.

The Methodist movement itself provided Wales with its first great romantic, William Williams, the hymn-writer, whose influence upon the subsequent literature of Wales has been of the greatest importance.

Political literature provides the names of Dr. Richard Price (1723–91), mathematician and philosopher who, though he had no profound influence on Welsh thought, had been born in Wales and educated in its dissenting academies, and the Rev. David Williams (1738–1816), citizen of France—both of whom were influenced by the ideals of the French Revolutionaries. In the same connexion, mention should be made of Morgan John Rhys, John Jones Glan-y-gors, Edward Williams (*Iolo Morganwg*), and Thomas Evans of Glyn Cothi. A significant feature in the history of the political and social reformers which had already been noted by one writer is that they also were to be found principally in those regions—the moorland fringe, the fall-line towns, industrial centres—which had provided fertile ground for the Puritan movement of the seventeenth century.

The Ancient Wisdoms

THE WOOD TURNER

He who knows the ways of beasts and birds,
Who can distinguish them by song and cry,
Who knows the bright quicksilver life in streams,
The courses that the stars take through the sky,
May never have laid hands to books, yet he
Is sharing wisdom with Infinity—
He who works with sensitive deft hands
At any woodcraft, will absorb the rain,
The sunlight and the starlight and the dew
That entered in the making of its grain;
He should grow tall and straight and clean and good,
Who daily breathes the essences of wood.
He who finds companionship in rocks,
And comfort in the touch of vine and leaf,
Who climbs a hill for joy, and shouts a song,
Who loves the feel of wind, will know no grief;
No loneliness that ever grows too great;
For he will never be quite desolate—
He shares, who is companioned long with these,
All ancient wisdoms and philosophies.

GRACE NOLL CROWELL

TURNERY
DESIGNS

*National Museum
of Wales
(Welsh Folk
Museum)*

Agriculture has always been of less importance on the Welsh uplands than in England, for the rain- and wind-swept uplands are better adapted for pasturage than for tillage, while in the large tracts that are in the rain-shadow area the gathering of crops in good condition is so uncertain and the soil often so sodden that the land, though often rich, can never be cultivated to its fullest extent. Sheep-farming, therefore, assumed a special importance in the eighteenth century for it gave rise to an intensive woollen industry carried on in the home and in small factories worked on the family principle. It was estimated by a contemporary observer that the trade in woollen goods from Merioneth and Montgomeryshire alone yielded over £60,000 a year. At the same time, the rural community was self-supporting in this as in most other directions, the itinerant tailors visiting almost every home to transform the home-made cloth into home-made clothes. Different parts of the country became associated with different types of cloth, with flannel or, as in the case of Bala, with a stocking trade.

Much of the internal commerce in the rural organization depended upon barter: labour, for instance, was requited with potatoes or butcher's meat, but the development of droving in particular led to the establishment of local banks which became still more necessary with the development of the woollen industry, mining and commercial ventures which necessitated the payment of weekly wages to employees.

In addition, however, to sheep-farming there was much stock-breeding in Wales while the eighteenth century saw many brave attempts at land-drainage and crop-cultivation. Several traces were to be seen of the effects of the Agricultural Revolution. Crop rotation and various agricultural implements were introduced and under the influence of enlightened landowners, such as at Hafod in Cardiganshire, Llangoed in Brecknockshire, and other places, foreign ploughwrights were prevailed upon to settle in Wales. Scientific cattle-breeding was encouraged and several attempts were made to improve the deplorable condition of the roads.

The eighteenth century was also to initiate movements which in the succeeding century were to transform large areas of the country into industrial regions. Down to the Industrial Revolution (with which we are not concerned here) the country had, in addition to the woollen industry, a variety of rural crafts which have not yet disappeared. Wood-turnery, practised at that time in many parts of the country, supplied the farmhouse and cottage kitchen with most of their utensils when earthenware, china, and metal-ware were known only in the houses of the wealthy. What earthenware there was came from the potteries on the fringes of the coal-measures, notably Ewenny in the Vale of Glamorgan and the Buckley district of Flintshire. Quilting was a home industry and quilted clothing persisted until later times in Wales than it did in England. The village smith, shoemaker, and carpenter supplied the iron-, leather-, and woodwork of village churches, chapels, farms, and cottages. The small ports of the country resounded with the noise of their shipbuilding yards which were to disappear in the nineteenth century with the advent of the railways. But it must be remembered that Anglesey at the end of the eighteenth century had the most important copper works in the world, while those at Swansea developed in the same period; the lead mines of Cardiganshire, Montgomeryshire, and north-east Wales were still worked; in the latter half of the century the slate industry of the north was developed and the same period saw the development of the iron industry of the south. But large areas of the Welsh coal-field which had no ironworks had to wait until the nineteenth century for the final destruction of their rural beauty.

Life on the Welsh moorland, however, preserved its continuity of tradition despite the inroads on its fringes of new methods, new movements, and new industries. His religious faith deepened and his language made still more secure, through the influence of the Sunday schools, the Welsh peasant was to achieve a standard of literacy and culture unknown in any other country except possibly parts of Scotland. As a peasant he conformed to immemorial custom: he married his sons and daughters with pagan rejoicings, mourned his dead with prehistoric ritual, and in the troubles of his simple life sought the advice of the 'conjurer' to undo the machinations of the country witches. He still commemorated the great feasts of the year with fitting decorum—All Hallows Eve, the New Year and the coming of Spring, Easter, Midsummer, and the saints' days. But with the developments of the nineteenth century the same peasant, still not forgetting his immemorial rites, could also discuss philosophy, religion, and science with a knowledge and a wisdom which betokened a rich and lasting culture. The next 150 years were to show how completely Tudor policy had failed, how impossible was any attempt to make English-men of Welsh men and that Wales was never to become merely a province of England. The first University College was established (at Aberystwyth) in 1872; the University of Wales received its Charter in 1893, the National Library and National Museum were founded in 1907. The setting up of the Welsh Folk Museum at St. Fagans during the years immediately following the Second World War is a final proof that the traditional culture of Wales has a contribution to make to world society.

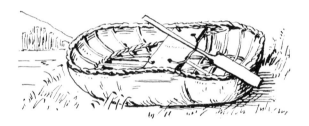

E. G. BOWEN

INDUSTRY

THE word industry is very often associated in our minds with congested grimy buildings, tall factory chimneys, coal mines, steel works, and railway sidings. Such scenes exist in parts of Wales as in many other countries whose rocks contain rich seams of coal. What we have to guard against is the notion that all the industries of a country are found on its coal-fields. This would be very far from the truth.

Although it actually employs less than a tenth of the total working population, agriculture is the basic industry of Wales. It is the oldest, and the most fundamental in so far as it helps to produce some of the raw materials of man's food and clothing. Taking Wales as a whole we find that its soils are generally heavy and cold, while moisture rather than sunshine and warmth is the outstanding feature of its climate. The pastoral character of Welsh farming is closely allied to this background. The differences in agricultural economy found from one part of the country to another are really dependent on relief. The lowland areas, especially in the east and along the northern and southern sea-plains, are largely devoted to mixed farming. Dairy cattle and sheep are pastured while most of the crops grown such as barley, oats, turnips, and potatoes are used either to feed the livestock or for consumption in the home. Milk production, however, is certainly the most important part of farming everywhere in the lowlands—an industry closely backed up by an assured national market provided by the Milk Marketing Board. The upland farm is, however, far more widespread in Wales than the lowland type, because the high land occupies such a large proportion of the country. Sheep rather than cattle occupy the uplands, but the farms often have a few cows, pigs, and poultry as well. A few acres of oats and potatoes may also be found. For many years agriculture as an industry in Wales was depressed and overshadowed by the heavy industries found on the coal-fields, but following upon the difficulties resulting from two world wars a marked change occurred. The industry has been rapidly mechanized for ploughing, reaping, sowing, milking and the transport of livestock and liquid milk. Every farmer has, in addition, his private motor car. In certain parts of the country where the climate is favourable early vegetables, especially potatoes, are a speciality. As a result of the demands all these developments make on garages and their mechanics as well as on the offices that have to keep the records, more people are employed in the small market towns than at any other time during the past century. This is clearly seen if we compare the population of representative market towns as recorded in the 1971 Census with the figures recorded forty years before.

At one time there were many other industries closely related to agriculture such as the woollen industry, the smithies, carpentry, saddlery, basketry, pottery, and other rural crafts. In many ways it can be said that wherever the countryside possessed rich mineral resources such as lead or zinc ore, slaty rocks, or good stone for quarrying or road-making, then the farmers would be engaged in mining or quarrying as well as working on their small-holdings. In other words, those industries were little more than rural industries in former times. The industrial revolution of the last century and the mass production of commodities that followed, together with the mechanization of agriculture, has practically killed all the older rural crafts. The lead and zinc mining areas of Cardiganshire and Montgomeryshire

THE RHONDDA VALLEY

Dixon Scott

and Flintshire are derelict. The slate quarries of Caernarvonshire and Merioneth are suffering severely from competition with synthetically produced tiles and earthenware goods generally. The quarrying of road metal alone flourishes, but even so the work is scattered among a very large number of very small quarries and the total number of men employed in Wales as a whole is not large. Some rural workers find employment with the Forestry Commission and others with the various schemes for water catchment and conservation. The coming of the motor-car has carried the tourist industry away from the seaside resorts more and more into the countryside and into the formerly secluded bays along the coast.

Wales has two coal-fields—one in the north-east and the other in the south. The south Wales coal-field is in fact the second largest in the whole of the British Isles. It can be divided into two sections, an eastern area which has bituminous coals and a western area with anthracite coals. The characteristic feature of the south Wales coal-field is the very high quality of the steam coals. As a result they are mined almost exclusively for export, and the fame of the south Wales coal spread the world over. Cardiff, Penarth, Barry, and Newport exported these coals. The anthracite coals of the western area are more suited for central-heating stoves and these coals have been sent overseas very largely to such countries as Scandinavia and Canada that have long severe winters and make great use of centrally

19

POTTERY KILN

heated buildings. These coals were exported through Swansea, Llanelli, and Burry Port. On the coal-field there are also two clearly marked metallurgical areas, one in the east and the other in the west, though they are not related in any way to the different types of coal. Both areas have important steel works. The older iron, steel, and tinplate works were located around Llanelli, Port Talbot, and Pontardawe in the west, and around Cardiff, Newport, Ebbw Vale, and the Afon Lwyd valley in the east, while in the Swansea area copper and nickel were also smelted. All the smaller works have now closed down and large hot and cold strip mills for the production of steel strip metal have been set up by the Steel Company of Wales at Port Talbot and again at Trostre and Velindre, near Llanelli. The Ebbw Vale works was one of the earliest in Britain to be converted into a continuous strip mill on American lines, while in recent years another mammoth strip mill has been built on the coastal flats at Llanwern, beyond Newport.

Blocks by courtesy of the National Museum of Wales

CIDER MILL

JOINTS AND STRATIFICATION IN A SLAB QUARRY,
BERWYN QUARRY, NEAR LLANGOLLEN, DENBIGHSHIRE

THE SURFACE OF A PEAT BOG, CORS GOCH, GLAN TEIFI,
NEAR TREGARON, CARDIGANSHIRE

Blocks by courtesy of the National Museum of Wales

OPENCAST COAL MINING, WAUNAFON,
BLAENAFON, MONMOUTHSHIRE

Although the northern coalfield is much smaller in size, it has, curiously, a greater variety of industries. The coalfield is long and narrow in shape. Its northern part in the former Flintshire has a long tradition of steel making, but is faced with changes at the present time. The western side of the Dee Estuary has the aircraft industry at Broughton, while rayon, chemicals and paper works are found at Flint, Holywell and Mold. The southern portion of this coalfield has seen a decline in coal and metal working although the steel works at Brymbo continues to function successfully by concentrating on special quality steels. In recent years important light industries have been concentrated at Marchwiel near Wrexham.

The most spectacular change that has taken place on the Welsh coal-fields, especially in south Wales, is the virtual eclipse of the coal-exporting trade in the inter-war years and particularly after 1945. This was caused not only by the disturbance of the coal markets during the war years but also by the development of oil and water-power resources as alternatives to coal in other countries. The eastern portion of the south Wales coal-field was naturally chiefly affected by this great change, but by and large its influence was widespread over both coal-fields. The efforts made to deal with the inter-war depression on the coal-fields are largely responsible for the startling industrial changes that have taken place during the last thirty years. These are the establishment of large trading estates like the ones at Treforest near Pontypridd or those at Hirwaun and Bridgend together with the general widespread scattering of the light industries—the latter include the making of imitation jewellery, carbon papers for typewriters, rubber goods, electric switch gear, clock- and watch-making. Such light industries were not dependent on coal but on electricity for their power supply. This in turn affected the mining industry. Coal was used to feed the power stations and this coal was not always derived from deep mining, but came from open-cast workings. The working of outcrop coal in this way was a new venture in modern times greatly assisted, of course, by highly developed mechanical scoopers and extractive machinery of all kinds. In recent years as the national electricity grid became more extensive, light industries have spread far and wide in the Welsh countryside. Many of the older market towns now tending to decay are turning to the light industries as a means of salvation. In this they are helped by local Development Councils and by the Government acting through the Welsh Development Agency and the Development Board for Rural Wales. The latter and its predecessors have been very active in Mid-Wales where the greatest impact is to be seen in the industrial estates at Newtown in Powys. Elsewhere advance factories have been directed towards such industries as car components, office equipment and special glasswork. A century ago the people flocked to the industries, but now the industries are being taken to the people.

While this is true of the foot-loose light industries, the heavier industries are still tied to the facilities the natural environment has to offer. This is particularly true of developments in recent years at Milford Haven. The advantages of bulk carriers for importing crude oil have led to the establishment of four massive oil refineries along the shores of this magnificent harbour where deep water allows tankers up to 250,000 tons to be berthed. The refineries are rapidly extending their capacities and crude oil is pumped overland from Milford Haven to Llandarcy near Swansea. It is estimated that a quarter of Britain's oilrefining capacity is located here. Another development utilizing a coastal site was the building of a smelter works for the British Aluminium industry at Amlwch in Anglesey. Here too a determining factor was the availability of deep water for importing aluminium, while electricity was obtainable from the nearby Wylfa nuclear power station. A company has also been established at Amlwch to utilize the sea water which is particularly suited to bromide extraction. It is clear that in future many sites along the coast of Wales will be used for the production of energy from oil, nuclear power and, in suitable areas, electrical power from the tides.

Literature through the Ages

I. THE EARLY POETS (c. 560–c. 1080)

IT has justly been claimed that Welsh is 'one of the great literary languages of the world'. The poets Taliesin and Aneirin flourished in the second half of the sixth century and lived in southern Scotland. The former sang the praises of his patron Urien and of Owain son of Urien while the latter composed a long poem commemorating the gallant war-band of 300 men who fell in a glorious but vain attempt to win back from the Saxons the old Roman fort of Catraeth (modern Catterick, in Yorkshire). These poets' compositions are typical heroic poetry in mode and matter and they show a great technical skill in the use of language and metre.

Very little poetry and hardly any prose have survived from the period between the seventh and tenth centuries. We have a few names of poets, and some fragments of verse which show that the heroic tradition persisted. Also from the latter part of this period are some nature and gnomic poems, some of them probably the work of anchorites, monks, and poets less professional than the recognized court bards. The nature poems are remarkable for their minute observation and concise expression. Some verse soliloquies and dialogues have survived from heroic sagas, with the prose narrative sections lost.

II. THE MEDIEVAL PERIOD

(a) The Court Poets (c. 1100–c. 1300)

During this period literature was composed mainly for the delight of the Welsh princes and their followers in the courts, each prince having his own court poet. Faced with the Norman invasion there was a great resurgence of the national spirit: there also arose great leaders such as Owain Gwynedd, Madog ap Maredudd of Powys, Llywelyn ab Iorwerth, and Llywelyn ap Gruffydd, and it is small wonder that their glorious deeds were acclaimed in poetry such as Wales has never since produced. There is a long list of poets of this period who celebrated the Welsh victories and exhorted their countrymen to yet greater glory. These poets had their own official place in the complicated hierarchy around the prince; membership of their ranks was restricted by certain conditions. Their apprenticeship was long and difficult, but it gave continuity of tradition, for the apprentice had to learn the *hengerdd* (ancient poetry) and an artificial diction far removed from contemporary ordinary speech. Their poems were chanted to the accompaniment of the harp. Gradually the elaborate system of *cynghanedd* (a combination of rhyme, alliteration, and consonancy) was developed much as it is used today for poems in the 'strict metres' as they are called, to distinguish them from the free metres, in which *cynghanedd* is not necessary.

Most of the poetry of this period consists of eulogies and elegies, and praise of the chieftain is conventionally fulsome. Different in matter but conforming to the same mode of expression and style are the religious poems on such topics as the saints, the terrors of Hell, the Day of Judgement, and repentance at the approach of death. Towards the end of this period there are a few love poems which gradually increased in number and were, in a sense, the precursors of one of the greatest poets Wales has ever produced—Dafydd ap Gwilym, of whom we shall speak below.

23

(b) Prose (c. 950–c. 1500)

Hitherto we have discussed only the poetry of Wales, which seems to have developed earlier than its prose. The Laws of Hywel the Good were codified towards the middle of the tenth century and in them Welsh prose is used to express unequivocally the finest distinctions of the legal mind in a very complex society. This in itself was no mean achievement. Another use of prose—that of entertainment—was made by the professional story-tellers. Their tales were traditional and their underlying material is mythology and folk-lore in decline, combined with heroic, pseudo-historical, and aetiological elements. Eleven such tales form the famous collection known as the *Mabinogion*, and of these the four called 'The Four Branches of the Mabinogi' are by far the best. Their 'author' was a fine stylist with a wide sympathetic understanding of human nature. The three tales known as 'the French Romances' show abundant evidence of Norman influence upon Welsh life in general and upon the native art of story-telling.

From the thirteenth century onwards there were many translations from Latin and French. Those from Latin include passages of Scripture, lives of saints, and various other texts, and those from French relate to the Charlemagne cycle of tales and the tales of the Holy Grail. Towards the end of the medieval period there were several translations from English, mainly in south Wales, which seems to have been the home of medieval Welsh prose. The development of prose as an artistic medium for story-telling outran its development as a medium of expressing the more abstruse facets of human activities. In fact, the prose writers of the Renaissance were painfully aware of this defect and, in order to remedy it, they consciously moulded a new type of Welsh prose which combined virility with artistry.

III. DAFYDD AP GWILYM AND THE CYWYDD POETS (*c.* 1300–*c.* 1650)

After the fall of Llywelyn, 'the last prince', in 1282 the patronage of the poets passed to the nobility, the heroic note was muted, and the complicated and jealously guarded canons of the court poets gradually declined. Dafydd ap Gwilym (*c.* 1325–*c.* 1380) and his followers took as their standard metre that of the *cywydd* which had been used hitherto by a lower class of poets. Dafydd sang of love and nature: but great though his delight was in the physical beauty of a maiden his deepest love is that of nature. His keen observation, minute description, and mastery of expression place him amongst the ranks of some of the great poets of medieval Europe.

Gradually the *cywydd* became the standard metrical form, and in the works of the great poets of the fifteenth century it reached a height of perfection which has never been surpassed. Its natural unit being the seven-syllabled couplet, it produced sparkling epigrams. There were set types of poems such as poems of contention, of supplication, and political prophecies. As time went on the teaching of the bards became less and less of a guarded secret and this eventually spelt the doom of the bardic organization in the joint upheavals of the Renaissance and the Reformation.

IV. MODERN PROSE (*c.* 1550–1960)

With the Renaissance there emerged a new type of prose which may be described as humanistic: its vocabulary and syntax were largely based on the language of the bards while its periods and cadences were influenced by classical models. It is seen in Salesbury's version of the New Testament (1567) and of the Book of Common Prayer (1567) as well as in Bishop William Morgan's version of the whole Bible (1588). These versions of the Scriptures were followed by other publications, mostly translations, in defence of the new religion or against it, the latter by Catholic exiles on the Continent. On the whole the Catholics cultivated a more popular style than did the apologists for the Reformation, but they had far less influence on later prose because Wales clung to its Protestantism. However, Catholics and Protestants were one in their efforts to mould a scholarly prose capable of expressing all the complex activities of the period. Later Puritan writers were more popular in their appeal but they sacrificed elegance of style. With the influence of the French Revolution and the writings of Tom Paine, publications of a new and revolutionary nature appeared, drawing more and more upon the resources of ordinary speech. Soon a reactionary movement set in, with Dr. W. O. Pughe as leader, to attempt to restore the literary standards of poetry and prose, but its pretentious style proved an adverse influence on Welsh prose for nearly a century. Towards the middle of the nineteenth century a simpler and better prose appeared. Attempts were made to use the novel as a literary form but prevailing religious and moral prejudices killed them. The only successful novelist was Daniel Owen, who gives a faithful picture of the Wales of his period. His characters ring true and his dialogue is natural and lively, but his 'plots' leave much to be desired.

Gradually, with the growth of scholarship, the glories of medieval and humanistic prose were rediscovered. The seventeenth-century classics were used as models, and their influence, combined with the living speech, has given Wales a modern prose which has strength and pliability. Many translations from French and German widened the literary horizon and new literary forms were adapted. The novels of Kate Roberts (as, too, her excellent short stories), those of E. Tegla Davies and T. Rowland Hughes, the short stories of D. J. Williams, T. Hughes Jones, and J. Gwilym Jones, the essays of T. H. Parry-Williams, T. J. Morgan, and F. G. Payne, the multifarious writings of W. J. Gruffydd, the literary and political essays of Saunders Lewis, the social essays of I. C. Peate, and the historical works of R. T. Jenkins—all these and many other works on scholarly subjects have found the new prose an adequate medium.

V. POST-RENAISSANCE POETRY (c. 1550–1960)

Although the old bardic organization failed to survive the Renaissance the old tradition of eulogy and elegy persisted, in an ever more debased form, well into the eighteenth century. In the late seventeenth and the eighteenth centuries there was a tendency to use the forms of folk-poetry to give moral counsel, as in Vicar Pritchard's *Canwyll y Cymry*. Thousands of ballads on all kinds of subjects, from religion to popular gossip, were written but their literary quality was very low. The Interludes of Twm o'r Nant (1739–1819) were far better, but they failed to develop into a modern drama. However, in the eighteenth century there came a revival of interest in the older poetry and that, combined with the influence of the English Augustan school of poets and critics, had a salutary effect on Welsh poetry. The eighteenth century also gave us the Methodist Revival, which in turn gave us Williams, Pantycelyn, the great hymn-writer, as its interpreter. His best hymns are perfect lyrics.

The Welsh Augustans, however, had rather a baneful influence on nineteenth-century poets, too many of whom tried to write a religious epic. Lewis Edwards (1809–87) encouraged the tendency to look beyond the confines of Wales, and gradually the influence of translations from Heine, combined with the songs of Alun and Ceiriog, produced the modern Welsh lyric, as seen in the works of Elfed and Eifion Wyn. There was an improvement, too, in the strict metre poetry, largely through the efforts of Sir J. Morris-Jones. The great figure of this new renaissance is T. Gwynn Jones (died 1949), but his disciple R. Williams Parry ranks close behind him. Both are essentially romantics. T. H. Parry-Williams, on the other hand, is scientific, individualistic, and introspective. Saunders Lewis and D. Gwenallt Jones are more concerned with the need for national and social unity. More popular poets are Crwys, Wil Ifan, Cynan, and I. D. Hooson, while I. C. Peate combines antiquarian interests with a fine feeling for form and technical finish. The younger generation of poets use *vers libre* (sometimes combined with *cynghanedd*), and stress the use of poetry as propaganda and as a form of expression for the non-rational elements in man. Modern poets like Alun Llywelyn-Williams, Waldo Williams, Euros Bowen, Bobi Jones, and Gwyn Thomas show that the poetic tradition is virile enough to express with artistry all the trends of contemporary life.

CELTIC CROSSES

1

REPRESENTATIVE

EARLY CHRISTIAN MONUMENTS

AND CROSSES OF WALES

2

3

4

26

1. THE GRAVESTONE OF CARAUSIUS (fifth century A.D.), from Pen-macho (Caern.)

2. CROSSED STONE (seventh century A.D.), from Llantrisant (Glam.)

3. CROSSED STONE (eighth century A.D.), from Strata Florida (Card.)

4. CROSSED STONE (ninth century A.D.), from Llangunnor (Carm.)

5. THE CROSS OF ENNIAUN (late ninth century A.D.), from Margam (Glam.)

6. THE CROSS OF IRBIC (late tenth century), from Llandough (Glam.)

7. SCULPTURED GRAVE-SLAB (late ninth century), from Meifod (Mont.)

8. THE GRAVE-SLAB OF HED AND ISAAC, sons of Bishop Abraham (1078–80 A.D.), from St. David's (Pemb.)

(Photographs by the National Museum of Wales. Blocks kindly lent by the Friends of Llandaff Cathedral)

8

5   6   7

R. L. CHARLES

WELSH PAINTING

W E cannot talk about the Welsh school of painting as we talk, for example, about the French school. Painting and sculpture are arts which thrive best in and around big towns, where artists can show and sell their pictures. Wales, until recently, has had no big towns: and her rich landlords, the artists' patrons, have mostly been English, at any rate in outlook. So Welsh painters have had to go elsewhere, and no tradition of painting has been able, until recently, to take root here. Today there are more painters working in Wales than ever before: but today we have not one school of painting, but many.

Nevertheless, the British school of painting has been notably enriched by Welsh artists during the last 200 years: and the mountains and castles of Wales have played a great part in its development. Since the far-off days of the eighteenth century, when people first began to admire picturesque scenery, Wales has been the happy painting-ground for almost all our leading artists.

It is right that their list should be headed by the Welshman Richard Wilson, the father of British landscape painting. A lifetime spent in London and Italy never dimmed his love for the land of his

PEMBROKE
TOWN AND
CASTLE
*by Richard
Wilson*

28

birth, and he returned to Wales to die. The subjects of many of his finest pictures are Welsh—Snowdon, Caernarfon, Pembroke. He lived in the eighteenth century, and was one of the original members of the Royal Academy. In his day, painted landscapes had to conform to certain rules, both of subject-matter and design. Wilson was the first great British artist to seek his living purely as a landscape painter: and one of the first in Europe to make the public feel that the pictures he painted were not only skilful arrangements of castles and trees and water and light, but also scenes which were dear to him.

In his picture of Pembroke, notice how the rocks and trees on the left are balanced by the deep shadow on the right; how they make a sort of frame for the Castle; how the composition is strengthened on the left by the little incident of the boys bird's-nesting; and how the eye is led back from foreground to background. And try to imagine the tender evening light which this reproduction hints at, and which pervades the whole picture and gives it such grandeur and peace.

John Gibson the sculptor was another great Welsh artist. He was born in Conway in 1790. He spent most of his life in Rome, and his statues are carved entirely in the manner and spirit of the works of ancient Greece and Rome. He lived at what then was the artistic centre of the world, and his work became famous throughout Europe. Other well-known Victorian artists of Welsh birth or descent were William Morris and Burne-Jones, the pre-Raphaelites, and G. F. Watts, the painter of portraits and allegories.

In modern times Wales has again nursed painters who are among the most famous of their day. Among these are Sir Frank Brangwyn, Augustus John, his sister the late Gwen John, and J. D. Innes, who died young. Augustus John is famous for his portraits, but some of his loveliest paintings are small 'Figures in Landscape', many of which were painted in north Wales. He has also painted many pictures of the gypsies with whom he once lived.

Modern artists often find it necessary to distort the natural appearance of things. Two artists who employ such methods in ways that somehow suggest the peculiar complications of Welsh poetry, and the spirit of Welsh legend, are David Jones and Ceri Richards. Another was the late Evan Walters: but his 'Welsh Collier' is a straightforward and striking portrait, and shows clearly his deep affection for the men among whom he grew up near Swansea.

ROMANY FOLK *by Augustus John*

A WELSH COLLIER *by Evan Walters*

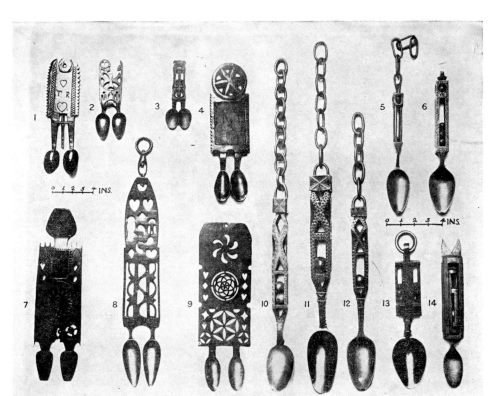

Welsh

Folk

Crafts

WELSH crafts have grown out of the
necessity for the peasant to make for himself the homely articles of daily use. The
art of the craftsman is to make these useful things
beautiful. He uses no elaborate apparatus and relies
usually on little more than a skilled pair of hands
and an eye for beauty of form. Sometimes the craftsman displayed his skill consciously, as when he made
a love-spoon just as another man might compose a
poem or a song. Then he became extravagant and
showed off his art in spoons with elaborate handles
and several bowls which are anything but useful.

Pottery was made in small factories and those at
Ewenny in Glamorgan have been at work since
the seventeenth century at the latest. Quilts on the
other hand were, and still are, made at home. The
stitching is not only decorative but is also essential
to hold the padding in position. The worker relies
on the accuracy of her own hand and eye in forming
the pattern. Samplers were at first merely examples
of new or attractive patterns and stitches—a kind of
pattern-book—but they were later put to decorative
uses as framed pictures, bed curtains, handkerchief
cases, &c., to show skill in embroidery.

Blocks by courtesy of the National Museum of Wales

POTTERY OF LATE EIGHTEENTH TO EARLY
NINETEENTH CENTURY, EWENNY, GLAM.

QUILT, MADE IN 1933, AT PORTH, RHONDDA, GLAM.

QUILT, DATED 1840, FROM CARDIGANSHIRE

SAMPLER 1823

SAMPLER 1780   WELSH

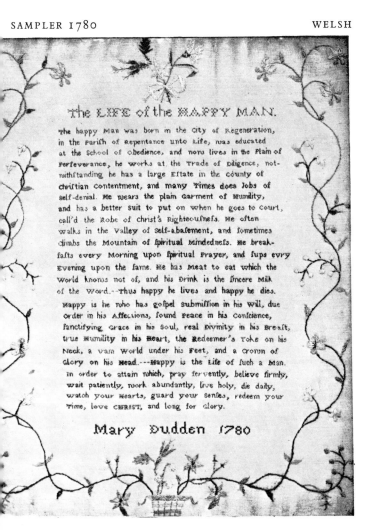

THE LIFE of the HAPPY MAN.

The happy Man was born in the City of Regeneration,
in the Parish of Repentance unto Life, was educated
at the School of Obedience, and now lives in the Plain of
Perseverance, he works at the Trade of Diligence, not-
withstanding he has a large Estate in the County of
Christian Contentment, and many Times does Jobs of
self-denial. He wears the plain Garment of Humility,
and has a better Suit to put on when he goes to Court,
call'd the Robe of Christ's Righteousness. He often
walks in the Valley of Self-abasement, and sometimes
climbs the Mountain of Spiritual Mindedness. He break-
fasts every Morning upon Spiritual Prayer, and sups evry
Evening upon the fame. He has Meat to eat which the
World knows not of, and his Drink is the sincere Milk
of the Word.--Thus happy he lives and happy he dies.
Happy is he who has gospel Submission in his Will, due
Order in his Affections, found Peace in his Conscience,
fanctifying Grace in his Soul, real Divinity in his Breast,
true Humility in his Heart, the Redeemer's Yoke on his
Neck, a vain World under his Feet, and a Crown of
Glory on his Head.---Happy is the Life of such a Man.
In order to attain which, pray fervently, believe firmly,
wait patiently, work abundantly, live holy, die daily,
watch your Hearts, guard your Senses, redeem your
Time, love CHRIST, and long for Glory.

Mary Dudden 1780

I Love them that love me and those that seek
me early shall find me Riches and honour are
with me yea durable riches and righteousness
My fruit is better than gold yea than fine gold
and my revenue than choice silver

Mary Williams her work Aged 11 · 1823

The Folk-Songs of Wales

ANYONE who would know the real spirit and heart of a people must needs know their folk-tales and folk-songs, and a rich heritage of these has fortunately been preserved in Wales. Some of the most haunting ones reflect the feelings of the people—their love and *hiraeth* and sorrow— as in *Titrwm Tatrwm, Mynwent Eglwys, Hiraeth, Lliw'r Heulwen, Pa le mae Nghariad i,* &c. Others show the farmer or the craftsman at his task, indicating sometimes in their rhythm the movements of the work. To this class belong the Oxen Songs of the Vale of Glamorgan, the blacksmith's song *Migldi Magldi* and the cobbler's song *Y Cobler du Bach.* Others again are songs to which Welsh people sang and danced when they met together, as they frequently did, to make merry. May Day was such a time of jollification. In an age when the year was divided into summer and winter only, winter beginning at Calan Gaea and summer at Calan Mai, it was only fitting that after the long dreary winter the beginning of summer should be heralded with song and dance. A relic of this has been preserved in the dance *Cadi Ha,* as well as in various songs. Many people in Wales have been fortunate enough to see as well as to hear the famous folk-singer, Robert Roberts of Tai'r Felin near Bala, singing his May song with its chorus—*Moliannwn oll yn llon,* to which the party accompanying him danced, or perhaps one should say, stepped. Bob Tai'r Felin, as he was called, had a store of unpublished songs—*Mari Glwyseg, Yr asyn a fu farw, Cân y Lleuen, Pwdin Pys,* &c., and many of these have fortunately been recorded. His singing was robust, virile, racy, and of the soil. He and his party were the last link between us and the days when people's feet could not help moving to the catchy rhythm of a native dance tune or chorus.

As in the folk-songs of other countries, Welsh folk-songs which belong to the realm of merry-making fall into well-known patterns. Songs with chorus abound, whether the chorus be on alternate lines as in *Y Gwcw Fach, Nos Galan, Torth o Fara,* or at the end as in *Y Gelynen, Ram, Robin Goch.* There are question-and-answer songs, such as *Yr Hen Wr Mwyn, Cyweiriwch fy Ngwely, 'Ble 'rwyt ti'n myned,* where there is an element of contest (*ymryson canu*) with a final flippant answer—occasionally by the woman, occasionally by the man. This *ymryson canu* or *pyncio* is also found in connexion with the custom still preserved at Llangynwyd in Glamorganshire—*Y Mari Lwyd,* when the men carrying the horse's head to the door engage in a rhyming contest with the women inside the house. Other songs which have the quality of a contest are the cumulative ones—*caneuon un ana'l*—as they have been called, since the cumulative part had to be sung all in one breath. When sung in this way, such songs as *Y Cyntaf dydd o'r Gwyliau, Un ac un o 'Mrodyr,* and the better known *Pren ar y Bryn* can be very exciting. The various forms of *Cyfri'r Geifr* (Counting the Goats) belong to this same class of singing games, with its question and answer and its tongue-twisting refrain.

Many of our finest hymn-tunes were originally folk-tunes. Some have remained almost unchanged, others have altered so much as to be almost unrecognizable. Reference should be made to the old Welsh carols, some of which have been published in a small volume, *Clychau'r Nadolig,* by W. S. Gwynn Williams and in a selection *Carolau Hen a Newydd* published by Undeb Noddwyr Alawon Cymru.

Some of the songs published in the eighteenth century by such men as the harpists, John Parry of Ruabon and Edward Jones (Bardd y Brenin) of Llandderfel, were undoubtedly old folk-tunes in origin, but in the main their collections contained varieties of harp-tunes and national airs.

The first volume of Welsh folk-songs proper did not appear until 1844. A prize was offered at the Abergavenny National Eisteddfod of 1836 for a volume of hitherto unpublished folk-songs with the words as sung by the people. This prize was won by Miss Maria Jane Williams of Aberpergwm in the Vale of Neath, and her collection was published in 1844 under the title *The Ancient Airs of Gwent and Morgannwg*. Here we find for the first time such well-known airs as *Y Deryn Pur*, *Y Fwyalchen*, *Bugeilio'r Gwenith Gwyn*, *Y Bore Glas*, and *Merch y Melinydd*, &c.

Other publications of folk and of national songs appeared in the nineteenth century, but taken as a whole this was a period when the natural delights of the Welsh people, including folk-songs and folk-dancing to the harp, were regarded as frivolities which should be discouraged. As a result of this attitude many songs have been lost, and in particular the Welsh dances have almost entirely disappeared. We now sing many of the old dance-tunes to words written by various poets and notably by Ceiriog, who knew the songs well and also was skilled in wedding words to music. Many tunes that might otherwise have fallen into disuse were thus preserved through the agency of his words.

Lively interest in Welsh folk-songs dates from the early years of this century. The Welsh Folk-Song Society was formed at Llangollen in 1908 for the purpose of collecting, publishing, and popularizing folk-music. Two years later the Society began issuing the *Journal of the Welsh Folk-Song Society*, and this publication has continued, with occasional breaks, up to the present day. These volumes, including folk-tunes, with their variant forms (all mercifully unarranged), with notes on them by various musicians and articles on folk-lore and custom, are of immense value to all who wish to become acquainted with Welsh folk-music.

Several names could be mentioned in connexion with the early years of the folk-song movement in Wales. Dr. Mary Davies did valuable pioneering work, which is too little known nowadays, but pride of place goes naturally to Dr. J. Lloyd Williams for his long life of service to Welsh folk-songs as collector, lecturer, writer, and particularly as a teacher. Under his guidance and inspiration at Bangor, a very large number of beautiful folk-songs, which might have been lost for ever, were discovered—and how interestingly very often—by members of 'Y Canorion'—a group which he formed for the purpose of collecting and singing these songs of the people. They have appeared from time to time in the *Journal*. Many of them were also published in the popular volumes by J. Lloyd Williams and Llew Tegid—*Welsh Folk Songs*, Parts I–III—where they are arranged for two or three voices. *Hwiangerddi Cymraeg*, by Lloyd Williams, a small volume of traditional nursery songs and lullabies, contains the well-known *Gee Geffyl Bach*, *Dacw Mam yn Dwad*, *Deryn y Bwn*, &c., which all Welsh-speaking children should take with them to school as a basis to build upon.

Many collections of folk-songs have appeared during this century. Tribute is due to Phillip Thomas of Neath for his great service to folk-music at the Welsh Summer Schools which were once such an attraction at Llanwrtyd Wells. The daily session given annually at this school to the learning of folk-songs under the direction of Phillip Thomas helped greatly to popularize these songs and to spread interest in them throughout the various localities from which members of the schools were drawn. A collection of over forty of these songs published by Phillip Thomas is now unfortunately out of print. Other collectors include Grace Gwyneddon Davies, Lady Herbert Lewis, Hubert Davies, and Enid Parry, all of whom have given invaluable service to the cause of folk-music. Several selections and arrangements of folk-songs have been issued by W. S. Gwynn-Williams, the author of *Welsh National Music and Dance*. Mention should also be made of the programme of folk-songs published annually under the auspices of *Undeb Noddwyr Alawon Cymru*, a booklet widely used in schools all over Wales and by branches of *Urdd Gobaith Cymru*. Through its camps, its week-end courses, its Eisteddfodau, and folk-festivals, its Celtic and international gatherings, *Yr Urdd* has given admirable service to the cause of folk-songs. Its young people are getting to know of the wealth of material available, and, what is of far greater importance, they sing the songs and enjoy them.

Through the agencies of schools, local and national Eisteddfodau, and festivals such as the annual Gŵyl Cerdd Dant, people generally are becoming more aware of the value and delights of folk-music.

MUSIC

Their instruments charm and delight the ear with their sweetness. . . . in their rhymed songs and set speeches they are so subtile and ingenious, that they produce, in their native tongue, ornaments of wonderful and exquisite invention both in words and sentences. Hence arise those poets whom they call Bards, of whom you will find many in this nation.

GIRALDUS CAMBRENSIS

PRESCELLY FROM THE MILL STREAM—MYNACHLOG-DDU

M. Wight

HILDA LL. WILLIAMS

Cultural Institutions

THE NATIONAL EISTEDDFOD AND THE GORSEDD OF WALES

Based on an article by Cynan, formerly Archdruid of Wales, in The Eisteddfod and The Gorsedd of Wales, published by The National Eisteddfod Council.

THE Eisteddfod is the best known of Welsh institutions, and there is nothing quite like it among any other peoples. Wherever there are Welsh people, there too, probably on St. David's Day, an eisteddfod will be held. On a much larger scale, and held during one week in August every year, we have our National Eisteddfod, to which many thousands throng, to participate, or else seek entertainment in the competitions in Art, Crafts, Music, and Literature. The Eisteddfod pavilion, specially constructed, holds up to 10,000 people, but is never adequate to accommodate the enthusiasts, nor is the whole week of competition the limit of its influence and interest. Intending competitors are hard at work throughout the year of the Eisteddfod either practising, or composing, or carrying out researches. The subjects for competition are many and comprehensive and include crafts associated with industry, ambulance work, choral and orchestral competitions, brass band contests, competitions in composing poetry and prose, drama (acting and writing), and many more. The National Eisteddfod thus covers most of those activities which go to make the rich pattern of Welsh culture. It is, at once, the inspiration and the test of worth, and its influence is incalculable. The whole proceedings are in Welsh, thus demonstrating as well as fostering the vigour and life of our language. One visit to the Eisteddfod, whether local or national, will convince a visitor of the reality of the Welsh language and of an essentially Welsh way of life.

The National Eisteddfod visits north and south Wales in alternate years, the choice of place being made and announced after considering rival applications from districts anxious to act as hosts. Even here there is keen competition and adjudication.

The Eisteddfod, as we know it, has grown from roots set in medieval times, but its present form is about a century old. The earliest recorded contest of poets and musicians was that held in Cardigan Castle in 1176, at which prizes of chairs were awarded to the winners. Thereafter there is no record of contests until the fifteenth and sixteenth centuries. In 1568 an eisteddfod was held in Caerwys, at which the following prizes were awarded: a miniature silver chair to the successful poet, a little silver 'crwth' to the winning fiddler, a silver tongue to the best singer, and a tiny silver harp to the champion harpist. This harp, only 6 inches in height, is a treasured survivor and reminder of those early attempts to encourage the advancement of the art and practice of music and poetry. Originally, the contests were limited to professional bards whose services were paid for by the noble families who kept them. It is of some interest that Queen Elizabeth, anxious that access to the homes of nobility should be possible only to bards of the highest standard, commanded twenty gentlemen of north Wales to examine and license bards. With the passing of time, the nobility became more and more English, and, therefore, less and less interested in the Welsh arts, and a deterioration of standard set in. That this was halted was due, in the first place, to the vision and energy of Thomas Jones of Corwen, who, seeing the potential power of the Eisteddfod for nurturing native culture, organized one at Corwen in 1789, to which the public were admitted for the first time. This eisteddfod was a great success in itself, but of greater importance was the fillip it appears to have given to the Gwyneddigion, a learned London Welsh society, to support regional eisteddfodau. This, in turn, led to a revival of interest in literature and music, and to the formation of other learned societies in Wales, who also supported eisteddfodau in their regions. In this way the movement progressed, if slowly, and standards of accomplishment and adjudication improved until, by now, success in the National Eisteddfod indicates substantial merit.

It was at one of these regional eisteddfodau in Carmarthen in 1819 that the Gorsedd first appeared. Like most other people, the Welsh had, and still have, an inordinate respect for the 'genuinely old' whether applied to things or to tradition, and the claim by Iolo Morganwg (bardic name of Edward Williams) that the bardic tradition in south Wales was druidic in origin was readily accepted. He founded 'Gorsedd Beirdd Ynys Prydain' (Gorsedd of the Bards of the Isle of Britain) in 1792 intending it to supplant the Eisteddfod. In this, however, he failed, and instead the two were merged, the Gorsedd holding the right of proclamation and of government. The Gorsedd still practises its right of proclamation; its pageantry and ritual provide much colour and dignity to the Eisteddfod, but its right of government is merged in the National Eisteddfod Council, and it no longer claims druidic antiquity. This National Eisteddfod Council is a development of the first committee set up in 1858 to organize the eisteddfod on a national scale, and the first so organized was that held in Denbigh in 1860. It was the first of the pattern to which the present festival belongs.

Members of the Gorsedd form the greater part of the membership of the Council, and thus the Gorsedd still exercises an important influence on the control of the National Eisteddfod. The aim of the Gorsedd is to 'ensure the co-operation of bards, men of letters, musicians and the patrons of the fine arts, in order to enrich bardism, literature, music and art in Wales'. It safeguards, too, the rites and customs of the bards and is governed by the Archdruid, elected from among the Druids to this high office for three years. Membership of the Gorsedd is normally by examination. A knowledge of Welsh is, of course, an essential qualification, even for honorary membership, except for members of the royal family or distinguished foreign artists and visitors whom Wales wishes to honour.

The Ovate Order is the first grade in membership, and is open to candidates by examination, and for honorary membership by proposal. Elevation to the second order of 'Bards, Musicians, and Literati' is possible only through examination, while the third grade—The Druidic Order—is reserved exclusively for those presented by the Druids themselves, and accepted by the Board as having made a substantial contribution of recognized distinction to Welsh Literature, Music, Scholarship, or Art. Robed according to degree, Ovates in green, Bards in blue, and Druids in white, the high officers wearing their symbolic regalia, the Gorsedd meets in public session to proclaim the following year's Eisteddfod at least a year and a day in advance. They assemble within a circle of massive stones arranged on the traditional plan. 'In the face of the sun—the eye of light' the protection of God is invoked, in this Gorsedd prayer, intoned in Welsh to the accompaniment of the harp:

Grant, O God, thy protection,
And in protection strength,
And in strength understanding,
And in understanding perception,
And in perception perception of righteousness,

And in perception of righteousness the love of it,
And in the love of it the love of all life,
And in all life to love God,
God and all goodness.

During the Eisteddfod itself, there are several such meetings and processions, and the Gorsedd takes part in the ceremonies of 'crowning' the poet presenting the best *Pryddest*,[1] and 'chairing' the poet

---

[1] A *Pryddest* is an ode in free metres.

presenting the winning *Awdl*.[1] The National Eisteddfod is much richer for this impressive pageantry, and is a force in the advancement of Welsh culture because of the expert interest and authority of the Gorsedd within the Eisteddfod Council.

THE NOSON LAWEN

The Noson Lawen is gaining favour as a form of entertainment on stage and radio. While this cannot be truly termed a revival, it has the merit of at least preserving some of the framework of a custom which dates back to the seventeenth century, when most of the farms were small and very isolated. The long days of summer gave little opportunity for community life, for sleep was the only respite from the long labours of the day. With the shorter winter days came more leisure, and the evergreen problem of how best to spend the evenings. The good-neighbourliness of those days led to gatherings in the 'big kitchen' of one of the larger farms and, in the comfort of a well-provided hearth, talk led to poetry, song, and dance, and formed the pattern of entertainment called 'Noson Lawen'. Penillion were sung to the music of harp and crwth—and later the violin. Sometimes this took the form of a competition when each singer in turn had to set verses to the air played, and in the metre and subject set by the first singer. Stories were told—including old folk-tales, fairy-tales, and ghost stories—and the younger members danced either in groups for the reels and jigs, or in individual Clog, Poker, and Trencher dances. All the while the women knitted; some of the young men carved love-spoons, and others fashioned elaborately carved shepherds' crooks. There was always plenty of refreshment, inevitably home-made, and, like the evening's fun, all the better for it.

The great religious revival of the eighteenth century produced an extremely puritanical outlook on life, and the Noson Lawen was frowned upon. This was the beginning of the decline of this delightful and typically Welsh institution, and, later, with greatly increasing transport facilities, it had to give way to the village concert, eisteddfod, and lecture, then to the cinema, radio and television. It has, however, enjoyed a new upsurge of popularity in recent years.

[1] An *Awdl* is a poem in the strict traditional metres of Welsh alliterative verse. There is no equivalent English form.

Welsh Proverbs

Aml bai lle ni charer.	It is easy to blame where there is no love.
Gwell un gair gwir na chan gair teg.	Better one true word than a hundred fair ones.
A heuo ddrain na cherdded yn droednoeth.	He who sows thorns should not walk barefoot.
A heuo ysgall ni fed wenith.	He who sows thistles will not reap wheat.
A ddywaid y peth a fynno *A glyw yr hyn nis mynno.*	He who says what he pleases Hears what does not please him.
Ni cheir gan lwynog ond ei groen.	A fox gives one nothing but his skin.

Some call it the pride of the morning,
And others a mountain mist,
When it lies on the hills at dawning
With the valley below sunkist—
When the coldness of night is over
And the light of the moon is done,
And hope lies still in the heart of
  the hill
For the day that has scarce begun.

HETHER KAY

E. J. Brown

Evan Evans. By courtesy of the Gower Society

I would seek rest in Gower,
Where fever calms and cools;
Rest on her moor-clasped beaches
Welling with easeful pools;
Rest in her old enchantment,
Rest in her sunset peace . . .
I will remember Gower
Till life and memory cease.

MELFIN JONES

GLYDER FACH

LLYN GWYNANT AND YR ARAN

CAERNARFON CASTLE

CNICHT

RHOSILLY BAY

CADER IDRIS

CASWELL BAY, GOWER

CITY HALL, CARDIFF

A WELSH COTTAGE

THE WELSH BORDER, RIVER WYE

SEVERN AT THE LONG BRIDGE, LLANIDLOES

RHEIDOL FALLS, NEAR ABERYSTWYTH

TINTERN ABBEY

COCKLE-GATHERERS OF FERRYSIDE

E. G. BOWEN

The Welsh Home

IT would seem that the Celtic people in Wales in prehistoric times lived either in the great hill-forts or in smaller fortified farmsteads. In either case they were not far removed from their cattle, and it is possible that in times of trouble and inter-tribal warfare everyone gathered within the great hill-forts together with their flocks and herds for defence. Many of the great hill-forts seem to take the form of a figure eight lying on its side, as it were, giving two marked lobes, in one of which excavations have shown the presence of hut dwellings, while the other lobe functions as a cattle kraal. There was always direct communication between the two lobes within the hill-fort itself.

In the post-Roman centuries in Wales it would appear that there was much forest clearing and that the people generally tended to move into the valleys. In this way more and more scattered settlements arose, and at that time, too, we think the earliest farm-houses were established. Most scholars today are of the opinion that these were originally arranged in a cluster, possibly around a small patch of arable land, but as one generation followed another it was essential that new farms were established, and so the settlement pattern became more and more scattered in type. Wales, therefore, differs markedly from England in the fact that there were no true villages. What approximated most closely to the nucleated English village in Wales in the early days was the gathering of houses around a chieftain's house, where his servants and retainers lived. Likewise, there were no towns in Wales. In almost every case Welsh towns represent an intrusive culture—brought in mainly by the Anglo-Normans. Geraldus Cambrensis, who travelled around Wales very extensively in the late twelfth century, tells us specifically that 'the Welsh have no towns'. As time went on, more and more fractionation of holdings naturally took place. Besides the large farm-houses themselves, cottages were set up along the roadsides or trackways or on the higher unenclosed ground. Some of the latter were, in the first instance, 'pirate' settlements representing what was, in fact, illicit squatting on the common land. It used to be the accepted tradition that if a newly married couple were in search of a home, they were permitted to go up to the common land, beyond the existing limit of settlement, on their wedding night, and if they and their friends could establish a cottage built of turf or clods of earth overnight, so that smoke was to be seen emitting from the chimney by dawn, then they could, in theory at least, claim the freehold of the site. It was said that the newly married husband was also permitted to throw his wood-axe in all directions from the newly erected homestead and that where it fell marked the perimeter of the land which the family were allowed to enclose. Such settlements were called *tai-un-nos*—'one-night houses'—and frequently they were given by the neighbours even more picturesque names such as 'Clod Hall' or 'Morning Surprise'. Later on, after the site had been established, the family would set about building a more permanent structure. In this way we have the origins of many of our present-day cottages and upland farms. The simple fact, therefore, is that in spite of our large cities like Cardiff, Newport, or Swansea, and our older market towns like Wrexham, Carmarthen, Haverfordwest, Caernarfon, Brecon, Dolgellau, Welshpool, and Newtown, and our large seaside resorts like Llandudno, Colwyn Bay, Rhyl, and Tenby, and indeed, our lesser village settlements such as Ponterwyd, Mynachlogddu, Tregaron, Caersws, Bontddu, or Talgarth, the traditional homes of the

OLD LONGHOUSE
CARMARTHENSHIRE

Llew Morgan

Welsh people consisted of the farmers' *tyddynod*, or farm-houses, and the numerous cottages that were scattered around. The latter housed the farm labourers, the cobblers, the tailors, the weavers, and the shoemakers, many of whose children went in turn to service on the farms. It should be remembered that these farms and cottages were not only the units of the settlement pattern that was characteristically Welsh, but they were the pivots of Welsh cultural life as well. In them was bred the love of singing, of poetry-making and recitation, together with the deep religious convictions that have characterized the people of Wales throughout the ages. Although there was a sharp distinction in social prestige between the farmer, proud of his ownership of land and (like the Hebrew patriarchs of old) of his flocks and herds and horses, and 'the people of the smaller houses' (as the cottagers were usually referred to), yet farmer and cottager formed one close rural community held together by many ties of language, religion, friendship, customs, and even, as we have seen, by economic dependence on one another. The smallholder not only sent his children to service on the farms but frequently possessed a few rows of potatoes or turnips in the farmer's fields. The 'gentlemen farmers' of Wales, as they were frequently called, had every reason to be proud folk. Very many of them were the descendants of the old native gentry and it is interesting to find in the early charters of the Welsh Princes (even before the end of the twelfth century, when making grants of land to churches and abbeys), the names of farmsteads that have survived in these localities to the present day.

We can now look a little more closely at a typical farm-house and cottage. Fig. 1 shows one of these farm-houses as it now appears in north Carmarthenshire. Originally, it had a thatched roof, and it is likely that the shed at the very end is a later addition. What is all important to note is that the animals and the humans are housed under the same roof. This is a characteristic feature of the Welsh long-house and many think that there we have a reflection of the very old tradition, going back to the Iron Age, when in the hill-forts the animals and the humans were together within the same enclosure. We get a glimpse of further detail by examining Fig. 2, which is a ground plan of a similar type of farm-house in the same county. The full length of the farm-house is sixty-one feet. If we entered by the door marked by the arrows we would find ourselves in a little entrance hall facing the dairy. If instead of going into the dairy we turned left we would enter the farm kitchen which was, in fact, the main

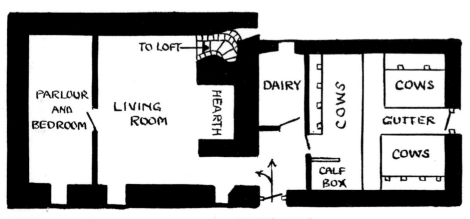

PLAN OF WELSH LONG-
HOUSE

(This drawing is made
from the one found in
The Welsh House by
Iorwerth C. Peate (1944), page 64)

living-room, where the family gathered after the day's work. On our right would be the hearth with its great fire-place and open chimney, eight feet wide, in which a log fire would be burning. Against the projecting wall of the hearth would be two wooden settles, one on each side on which the farmer and his wife sat together with their children and the farm servants. There was no distinction between master and man in the old Welsh home, each called the other by their Christian names and the servant never referred to his master as 'boss', or addressed him as 'Sir'. It is also significant that the hearth from time immemorial was the central place in the home—the pivot around which the household turned. Modern excavations have shown that the fire-place was always located in the centre of the huts in the early Iron Age hill-forts. If you looked up at the wooden ceiling with its great oak beams you would see bunches of dried herbs hanging, together with two or three bacon hams and a similar number of flitches and almost certainly a bladder of lard. On the walls around would hang the farmer's gun and the horse stirrups and an array of brasses belonging to the best harness. In most of these old farm kitchens there persisted a tradition (possibly again going back to the Iron Age huts) of building a raised platform some six inches high, some two and a half feet wide, above the kitchen floor. On this was placed the long-case clock and the dresser filled with the family china, while in a corner would be found a triangular-shaped cupboard, which fitted against the walls, containing the smaller china— cups and saucers and fancy pieces. In the far corner of the room were a series of stone steps leading up to the loft—a triangular space between ceiling and roof in which the servants slept. The farmer and his wife in olden days slept on the ground floor in the room adjacent to the living-room, which was also used as a parlour and usually contained, as well as the bed, a chest of drawers and a round table on which the family Bible was placed. In modern language it would be described as 'a bed-sitter'. If we now retrace our steps to the door by which we entered and turn right rather than left we would enter the *beudy*, or the cow-stalls with gutters between the stalls for drainage purposes. Most of these 'cow-sheds' (as they are now called) had a little calf-box conveniently placed in one corner, as the diagram shows. This whole section of the farm-house in which the animals dwelt was always referred to as 'the lower end of the house'. So far we have described the layout of a typical Welsh farm-house before later changes were made. These belong in most instances to the nineteenth century. Then the farmer frequently decided to raise the living quarters so that it had a separate door to enter and space upstairs for at least three bedrooms in front and often two more behind. Better chimneys were added and the whole farm-house roofed with slates instead of thatch. Downstairs in this new arrangement (Fig. 3) the kitchen and living-room was usually on the left and the parlour on the right, while in the hall you faced the stairs leading to the bedrooms on the first floor. Frequently there was a 'lean-to' shed built behind the house as a dairy and entered from the kitchen. It will be appreciated that these later changes have in no way altered the pattern of the Welsh 'long-house'—the animals and the humans are still

WELSH FARM-HOUSE

Brython Press

THATCHED COTTAGE

D. Parry Jones

under the same roof. In certain parts of Wales distinctive styles of building are to be seen without any real change of basic plan. The most spectacular of these local building techniques is the magnificent 'black and white' timber-framed houses found in eastern central Wales, especially in the valley of the upper Severn and its tributaries.

The old Welsh cottages (now largely disappeared or in ruins) were very simple one-storey, two-roomed structures. They were in most cases 'home-made' in the sense that they were built by the people who first occupied them without any technical help from outside. Their only assistance came from their neighbours. Wherever they are found they appear to be constructed very much as the *tai-un-nos* were. The walls were built of a yellow sticky mould—very often it was the wet boulder clay soil of the fields, which was mixed with moss, straw, and hair and then pounded until it acquired the consistency of mortar. It would appear that it was built up layer by layer with an interval of time left between each layer for the material to harden and dry. When the walls reached the required height the beams were placed in position and a thatched roof placed overall. The roof was seldom high enough to permit a loft between the ceiling and the rafters. The interior partition walls which separated the living-room from the bedroom and parlour were made of wattle, thick pliable sticks interlaced between fixed posts and then covered with clay and whitewashed and later covered with wallpaper. There were often two small partition walls running parallel to each other, thus allowing a passage-way into the cottage from the front door, with doorways through them into the living-room and bedroom-parlour respectively. The outside of the cottage, too, was invariably whitewashed, while flowering plants and creepers adorned the frontage (see Fig. 4, which shows a typical cottage of this kind near Lampeter in Cardiganshire). It is important to remember that these little cottages adorned the country-side. They fitted perfectly into an environment where peace and culture reigned unmolested. A. G. Bradley has said that 'Carmarthenshire and still more Cardiganshire boasts of the quaintest and most picturesque thatched cottages in the world . . . the roof is a thing of joy and a work of art that throws the thatched cottages of Devon and Northamptonshire . . . hopelessly into the shade'. How much darker, for example, is the shadow that has fallen on those far-away American megalopoles (which received so many of their inhabitants originally from these Welsh cottages) or, for that matter, on our own ungainly urban sprawls?

Sources. I. C. Peate, *The Welsh House—A Study in Folk Culture*, Liverpool, 1944, and D. Parry-Jones, *Welsh Country Upbringing*, Batsford, London, 1948.

J. A. DAVIES

Education in Wales

AT the beginning of the nineteenth century the provision of educational facilities in Wales at all levels was extremely meagre. The Circulating Schools which had been established by the Revd. Griffith Jones of Llanddowror in the eighteenth century were justifiably famous and the development of the Sunday School movement was equally powerful, though the educational work of both had severe limitations, as the Circulating Schools embraced adults as well as children and the Sunday Schools' work was obviously primarily religious. They gave to the people of Wales a knowledge of the language which was used to read the Bible in the magnificent prose of the sixteenth-century Bishop Morgan. They were taught to read but not to write.

Early in the nineteenth century two societies were formed in England to promote the education of the poorer children. One of them was the British and Foreign School Society (1808) and the other the National Society (1811). Whereas the National Schools were to teach the religious principles of the Church in England, religious teaching in the British Schools was to be entirely undenominational. In the latter half of the nineteenth century National, British, and Voluntary Schools were opened in large numbers, but even so only a small minority of the children of Wales were being educated in the 1860s; and as education was not yet compulsory or free, their attendance was very irregular.

The first general Education Act of 1870 increased Government grants to the Voluntary Schools and declared that new schools should be built wherever they were needed. As a result of the Act of 1870, hundreds of Board Schools were built in Wales, and in 1880 another Act was passed which made it compulsory for all children to attend school until they were 13. School fees were abolished in 1881.

Wales was now provided with a system of elementary schools that covered the whole country. But though these schools did much to instruct their pupils, the language, the literature, the history, and the geography of Wales were almost completely ignored. By the third quarter of the century there were four Teacher Training Colleges established together with the University College of Wales, Aberystwyth, so that the provision of an extensive system of elementary education had been assured. The Welsh Intermediate Act of 1889 meant that secondary schools were established in Wales a decade before similar provision was made in England. The Central Welsh Board was formed to be responsible for examining and inspecting these new schools in an attempt to set common standards throughout Wales. University Education was catered for by the founding under Royal Charter in 1893 of the University of Wales. The University is a federal University and originally consisted of the University Colleges at Aberystwyth, Bangor, and Cardiff. The University College of Swansea was a later addition, as was the Welsh National School of Medicine at Cardiff. In 1967 the former Welsh College of Advanced Technology was incorporated as a constituent college of the University with the title 'University of Wales Institute of Science and Technology'. In 1971 St. David's College, Lampeter, also became part of the federal University of Wales.

There were two significant developments during the first half of the present century: the creation of the Welsh Department of the Board of Education in 1907 and the growth of the Central and Senior Schools for those children who would benefit from a less academic and more practical curriculum.

AN OLD
PRIMARY SCHOOL

Mont. L. E. A.

NEW PRIMARY
SCHOOL WITH
COMMUNITY
CENTRE

Mont. L. E. A.

By the middle of the present century the Butler Act of 1944 made Secondary Education compulsory for all over 11 years of age and insisted on equality of amenities and equality of opportunity. It was a great challenge to the Welsh Authorities—a challenge which was eagerly accepted. The Chairman of one of the Welsh Authorities welcomed the Act in these words:

'Although we in Wales have been proud of our progressive ideas on education we have, nevertheless, for many years been conscious of the shortcomings of our system. We therefore welcomed the Butler Act of 1944 with great enthusiasm and every Education Authority in Wales set itself eagerly to the task of preparing plans to meet the demands of the new legislation. . . . It is our task to legislate for the future. This is a serious responsibility but let us legislate boldly.'

The new Nursery, Primary, Secondary, and Technical Schools, Colleges, Community Centres, and Youth Centres which can be seen everywhere in Wales today are ample proof of the desire of the Welsh Authorities to provide the very best facilities for the young men and women of Wales.

There are three stages in the present educational system: Primary, Secondary, and Further (including Higher) Education. The years of compulsory schooling are from 5 to 16—the minimum leaving age established in 1970. The transition from Primary to Secondary School is made at about the age of 11. Further Education is voluntary and includes Technical Colleges, Adult Education, and the Youth Service as well as the University and Colleges of Education. Children under the age of 5 may be provided for in Nursery Schools or in Nursery Classes attached to Infant Schools. Special educational provision has to be made for children who cannot benefit from the education given in the ordinary schools, such as children who are deaf, blind, physically handicapped, educationally subnormal, or maladjusted.

In December 1946 the Minister of Education accepted the recommendations of a working party that a Joint Education Committee should be established to meet the educational needs of Wales as a whole, through the combined action of all Welsh Local Educational Authorities. The Welsh Joint Education Committee thus provides the machinery for securing, by co-operation and unity of action, a system of education in Wales which suits the special needs of the children in Wales.

In Wales the responsibilities of the Department of Education and Science are looked after by the Education Office for Wales, whose headquarters are in Cardiff. The Education Office for Wales works in close consultation with the Office of the Secretary of State for Wales. Government responsibility for the University is exercised, as in the case of all British universities, through the University Grants Committee. A new independent body, 'The Schools Council for the Curriculum and Examinations', came into existence in 1964. This represents the whole educational service, including the University, the Department, and Her Majesty's Inspectorate, the majority of the members being practising teachers. Its role is to promote curriculum study and development and to sponsor research and inquiry.

The Secretary of State made a general request to education authorities in 1965 to introduce comprehensive education in accordance with the Government's declared objective to abolish separatism in secondary schools. Comprehensive Secondary Schools are schools which take in all the pupils of secondary school age from a given area. All the Welsh Authorities have been active in implementing the comprehensive principle. In recent years there has been a significant growth in the number of bilingual comprehensive schools and the number of pupils attending them.

The schools of Wales are conscious of their double responsibility in a dynamic and rapidly changing society—to equip their children with the qualifications they will need to earn their living in a technological age and, on the other hand, with the development of human personality in a bilingual society.

It is a winter's tale
That the snow blind twilight ferries over the lakes
And floating fields from the farm in the cup of the vales,
Gliding windless through the hand folded flakes,
The pale breath of cattle at the stealthy sail,

And the stars falling cold,
And the breath of hay in the snow, and the far owl
Warning among the folds, and the frozen hold
Flocked with the sheep white smoke of the farm house cowl
In the river wended vales where the tale was told.

DYLAN THOMAS

1

2

3

1. CRAFTWORK—Making a canoe

2. ON THE LAND—Youth at the wheel

3. TECHNICAL EDUCATION—Electrical welding

4. ACTIVITY GROUP—Netball competition in a youth centre

5. DAY RELEASE CLASSES—Engineering students

6. THE COMPUTER—Work of the day

7. MECHANICS—Instruction in tractor repairs

8. CARPENTRY—An evening class in action

4

5

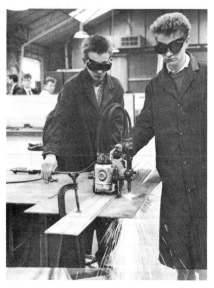

6

7

8

THE UNIVERSITY COLLEGE OF WALES,
ABERYSTWYTH

THE UNIVERSITY COLLEGE OF NORTH WALES,
BANGOR

THE NATIONAL LIBRARY OF WALES

THE NATIONAL MUSEUM OF WALES

THE UNIVERSITY COLLEGE OF SOUTH WALES
AND MONMOUTHSHIRE, CARDIFF

THE UNIVERSITY COLLEGE OF SWANSEA

CAMPING—A most popular outdoor activity included in many summer programmes

COUNTRY SKILLS—A rural youth group in a sheep-shearing competition

DRAMA AND ART—Youth groups take up dramatic work with enthusiasm, sometimes also making and painting the set required. Some make their meeting-places gay and colourful

A CLUB SINGS—All over Wales members of the Youth Movement sing—some for the joy of it, others to take part in an Eisteddfod or concert

MOUNTAIN RESCUE WORK—A team goes into practise— First aid and rescue work is studied in a practical way by different organizations

BRIDGE BUILDING—Mixed activities are popular in many clubs. This photograph shows a pulley being fixed at an all-Wales camp

B. J. GRIFFITHS

The Youth Service in Wales

At the beginning of this century and, indeed, until the end of the First World War, education in Wales was very formal and largely dependent on books and there was a sharp distinction between school work and play. Leisure-time activities were unorganized and what was available was centred on the churches and chapels. Furthermore, the aftermath of the Industrial Revolution created such a great demand for clerks and office staff for industrial concerns and other establishments that much of our formal education was for a position in life and the white-collared clerical posts were much coveted positions. Apart from the 'night schools', as they were called, which offered some further education of a technical nature to the keen young people, there was little to do after formal school hours but to attend church or chapel activities or walk the streets. Long before the Government and Local Education Authorities took an interest in Youth Service we must recognize the enormous contribution made by the voluntary organizations, of which the Y.M.C.A., the Scouts, the Guides, and Church groups were among the earliest, and later, in Wales, Urdd Gobaith Cymru (the Welsh League of Youth).

After the last war the Youth Service provided by the Local Education Authorities gained considerable momentum and Wales, in spite of our somewhat conservative tradition in this field, very quickly recognized the importance of social and cultural education as distinct from the traditional formal education of the past; County Youth Committees were set up and it was only natural that such committees would wish to include in their youth work many of the significant elements of the traditional cultural pattern of Wales. The eisteddfod is an integral part of this pattern and has been used by the Youth Service to foster worthwhile activities. In this way opportunities have been provided for young people to become interested in music, drama, and the arts.

One of the most interesting features of the Welsh pattern is that, just as in the Sunday Schools in the past, leisure provision is not confined to young people. The report on 'Post-war Youth Service in Wales' pointed out that the social and recreational facilities provided should not be confined to adolescents; it should be continued through adolescence into adult life and a general 'leisure service' should be developed for all age groups. The principle was accepted that the whole community needs provision for healthy, positive leisure-time activities as a permanent service. It is not surprising, therefore, that most of the Youth Service Officers employed by Local Education Authorities in Wales are also responsible for some aspects of adult education and community service. In some areas Local Education Authorities have set up 'adult and youth' centres, where one warden is responsible for both sections. There is, therefore, a close link between all aspects of post-school work in Wales and this helps to link the work of youth organizations with the community in which they live.

Since 1960 there has been an increased interest in outdoor activities. The Welsh countryside with its hills, mountains, and coasts is exceptionally well suited to outdoor activities and a recent survey made by the Central Council of Physical Recreation underlines the fact that more and more young people in Wales are now being attracted to outdoor pursuits. Team games have always been well catered for by the Youth Service, but such activities as rock climbing, mountaineering, sailing, and

51

A COMPETITOR AT THE NATIONAL YOUTH
ATHLETICS MEETING

caving are newcomers in the work of Welsh youth organizations. In addition, many local Education Authorities and voluntary organizations are now planning new outdoor pursuits centres; there has also been a greater recognition of the value of single activity groups. The Duke of Edinburgh's Award Scheme has stimulated such activities and its place in the development of outdoor youth activities is a contribution of the first importance.

An additional feature in the youth work in Wales was the foundation in 1945 of the National Youth Orchestra of Wales. This orchestra has given a concert at the Royal National Eisteddfod of Wales every year since 1948, has taken part in other festivals, and has undertaken concert tours in overseas countries. The orchestra is maintained by the eight Local Education Authorities and is administered on their behalf by the Welsh Joint Education Committee. A three-week course and concert tour is held every summer, and competition for places in the orchestra is extremely keen; all the players are under 21 years of age. Most of the members of the orchestra continue with their interest in music and become active members of adult amateur orchestras and a small proportion become professional musicians and find places in well-known British orchestras.

These new patterns have not developed as something apart from traditional formal education as such; a close link between the two has been a special feature of Wales. A large proportion of the part-time leaders, both paid and unpaid, is drawn from the teaching profession, enabling some interesting educational group work to be carried on in many centres and clubs. Clubs and centres have been established in secondary schools, sometimes in specially planned youth wings, and some interesting experiments have emerged, showing that activities can be linked for the mutual benefit of school and youth club. In spite of this close link it should be remembered that only slightly over one-half of the part-time leaders employed by Local Education Authorities and voluntary organizations in Wales are qualified teachers. Much, however, still depends on the good service rendered by the unpaid and, indeed, untrained helpers. There is a great scope here for young people to volunteer as leaders; to remember how much has been done for them by the Youth Service so that they, in turn, should accept the challenge and do something for the young people of their own generation. This challenge is being taken up in Wales and recent events reveal a widespread interest. A conference held in Cardiff recently to consider the establishment of training agencies for part-time youth leaders was attended by representatives of the four University Institutes of Education, the Department of Education and Science, all Local Education Authorities and Voluntary Youth Organizations in Wales; which exemplifies the partnership that exists in Wales in the field of youth work. Eight training agencies were established and training courses were initiated to cater for all areas in Wales. The response has been very encouraging and all agencies have received more applications for training than can be accepted. These agencies have also

THE NATIONAL YOUTH ORCHESTRA
OF WALES

met to confer on methods of training and to consider the problems which have arisen in making provision for basic courses for part-time youth leaders.

No statement concerning youth movements in Wales is complete without mentioning the dual problem presented by the distribution of the population, and its bilingual character. With two-thirds of the total population gathered in the south-eastern quadrant, considerable areas in Upland Wales are very sparsely populated and, indeed, are suffering from continuous depopulation.

In recent years some Local Education Authorities in the rural areas of Wales have been considering the provision of better facilities for young people in isolated communities. It has been found that the pattern of youth service provided in urban communities is not always suitable for sparsely populated areas. It is not possible to provide adequate facilities in all villages because of lack of leadership and the small number in any one age group. Some interesting experiments have been made by certain Local Education Authorities and these include providing an annexe to a rural primary school which serves as a community centre for adults and young people; encouraging and helping adult societies to form youth sections; providing area youth clubs which are situated at focal points suitable for neighbouring villages; and setting up special activity clubs for groups drawn from a fairly wide area, since young people who live in the country are more mobile today than ever before. These experiments have been made in areas which have suffered severely from rural depopulation, and the results of these experiments will, it is hoped, help to stem the drift from the countryside.

The bilingual character of the population necessitates a special approach to the problems of youth and at the same time multiplies them. It is, likewise, obvious that a bilingual nation needs bilingual provision in its youth clubs as in its schools. It is true that only a minority of the young people of Wales now speak Welsh, but those who do not are none the less Welsh in sentiment and thus the Youth Service in Wales must provide opportunities for all young people to learn something of their cultural heritage. In this way they can be helped to find themselves; understanding something of their environment, and making a full contribution to the life of the community.

When will it come, that golden time,
When every man is free?
Men who have power to choose their tasks
Have all their liberty.

They'll sweat and toil who love to feel
Their muscles swell and move;
While men whose minds are more to them,
Create the dreams we love.

When will it come, that golden time,
When every heart must sing?
The power to choose the work we love
Makes every man a king.

W. H. DAVIES

Justin B. Ingram

HIGH DIVE FROM DIPPING BRIDGE

The 'Dipping Bridge' at Merthyr Mawr in the Vale of Glamorgan crosses the Ogmore river. Farmers have driven their sheep here for washing for generations. Years ago flocks were brought in such numbers from all over the countryside that it was difficult to arrange for them to take their turn. Although seldom in use now the old methods are still carried out. A flock is driven on to the bridge and fastened there with improvised gates. Each sheep in turn is then pushed through the hole in the parapet to take its plunge into the water below. Once over the shock and short swim across the river they climb out fresh and clean after their dip. The victims rarely swim the wrong way but if they do the ever watchful sheep dogs reluctantly take to the water to guide them to safety.

E. G. BOWEN

Welsh Place-Names and the Welsh Language

WE know that Celtic-speaking peoples entered the British Isles from the Continent in large numbers in the late Bronze Age and during the Iron Age—that is between 750 and 75 B.C. Many scholars think that the earliest immigrants spoke dialects of Celtic speech that used QU or Q sounds, like the Irish word *quinc* for the numeral five. The Irish, Gaelic, and Manx languages belong to this group. It is thought that the later Celtic immigrants brought with them dialects of Celtic speech which gave rise to Welsh, Cornish (now extinct), and Breton. These later invaders used P sounds as found in the word *pump*—the Welsh word for the numeral five. This is the story of the P and Q Celts. Thus it was that immediately before and after the Roman occupation of Britain all of what is now Wales was Celtic in speech, and in marked contrast to Irish, Manx, Gaelic, and Cornish, Welsh has remained an active and virile language and is still spoken by more than half a million people in Wales. Spoken Welsh is very pleasing to the ear and is above all else the language of poetry and song and equally well suited to elegant prose, as is clearly seen in the magnificent translation of the Bible into Welsh in the age of Queen Elizabeth I. It was this translation that did so much towards the preservation of the language in the succeeding centuries. Furthermore, the Celtic people generally have a deep sense of place and the place-names they use are worth understanding. A knowledge of Welsh place-names can be a source of great delight and of great assistance in the proper understanding of both the people and the countryside.

Welsh place-names are not so difficult to pronounce as the array of consonants that usually compose them would seem to suggest. Once the elements are mastered, the process is easy and reliable, because Welsh is a much more phonetic language than English and the sounds represented by the letters are, on the whole, very consistent. It is, however, impossible to utter Welsh words with English sounds. Much of the difficulty that English speakers experience with Welsh names arises from the failure to appreciate this fact. The Welsh alphabet has several letters or symbols not found in English, such as: ch, dd, ff, ng, rh, and ll, of which the most difficult to pronounce is the last one—ll. It can best be attempted by closing the teeth and pressing the tongue well forward, opening the mouth and breathing outwards to make almost a hissing sound. The symbol occurs in the frequently used Welsh place-name prefix *Llan*—(which now means 'a church', but originally meant a 'religious or small monastic enclosure'). Since Wales was converted to Christianity in the early post-Roman centuries by wandering monks, or 'saints', as they are often called, we frequently find the name of the particular saint (or that of his immediate patron) still attached to the church or *Llan* which he originally founded. The church, in turn, gives its name to the village that grew around it, so names beginning in *Llan* occur very frequently in Wales. This is true of other Celtic lands as well wherever the Celtic saints spread, although the prefix might be Kil—or Kill in Ireland, and Keill in the Isle of Man. Since it is clear that the Celtic saints played a very important part in laying down the ground-work of the place-name pattern in Wales it is worth saying a little more about them. These wandering monks would select what they thought was a convenient preaching centre and set up a preaching cross there. If things turned out favourably, a small wattle-and-daub church would be erected, and a few beehive huts set up for the saint's immediate followers—the whole being enclosed within a great earthen wall or rampart as a protection against man and beast. This was the original *Llan*. Later on, if things continued to progress the wattle-and-daub church would be replaced by a wooden structure and ultimately by a stone building. The tomb of the original founder would attract pilgrims and worshippers, and slowly a nucleation of houses would gather around the church and a tiny village would grow up, and if the settlement was well placed in relation to modern conditions, a fully grown town would arise still bearing the saint's name. In this way Llanbadarn, Llandeilo, and even Llandudno originated. Sometimes, however, especially when the saint had gone to seek solitude and retire from the world and select a very remote site, nothing would happen. He would have set up his cell in some inhospitable place, on an island, or the edge of the cliffs, or on a bare mountain side—places that would not attract permanent settlers and so very often the little church decayed, or remains, as so frequently happens in Wales, all by itself in the landscape. In the case of the three place-names we have already mentioned their literal meaning is 'the church of Padarn', 'the church of Teilo', 'the church of Tudno' respectively, but the reader can see at a glance that we are here brought face to face with yet another major difficulty in attempting to understand Welsh place-names correctly. This is the mutation of the initial consonants which occurs when elements are compounded such as *Llan* and the founder's name.

By mutation of the initial letter Padarn becomes Badarn in Llanbadarn, and Teilo becomes Deilo in Llandeilo, and Tudno becomes Dudno in Llandudno. It is impossible to give in such a short statement as this all the rules to be followed in Welsh initial consonant mutations, but here are a few of them as they occur in place-names. They will suffice to indicate how complicated the mutational system is.

The initial consonant of a feminine singular noun is softened after the definite article as in Pen-y-bont (Pen+y+pont) meaning literally 'the head of the bridge'. The initial consonant of the noun is also always softened after the preposition *ar*, meaning *on*, as in Pontardawe (pont (the bridge) + ar (on)+ Tawe (the name of the river)). When the preposition *yn* (in) is used the initial consonant suffers nasal mutation as in Llanfair-ym-Muallt (Llan (the church) + Mair (Mary) + yn (in) + Buallt (the name of a district in Breconshire)). Then again the initial consonant of an adjective undergoes a soft mutation after a feminine singular noun, as in the place-name Ynyslas in North Cardiganshire (Ynys (island)+ glas (green)). In this case the soft mutation involves the omission of the 'g' in 'glas'. We can look at one final example where the initial consonant of a second element of a compound also undergoes a soft mutation as in Brithdir (Brith (speckled) + tir (land)).

In order to appreciate another fascinating aspect of Welsh place-names we need to look further back into prehistoric times than the period of the coming of the Celtic peoples themselves. When the Celtic people arrived in what is now Wales they found people already there—people who came in the Bronze Age and even in the preceding Neolithic Age. These early people had given names to many of the rivers and hills and mountains, and these older (pre-Celtic) names were taken over by the Celts and so have come down to us today. We are familiar with them on our maps, and in everyday speech, but we do not know what they 'mean'. Look at some of the river names in Wales—the Tywi, the Teifi, the Ystwyth, the Rheidol, the Tawe, the Nedd, the Dyfi, the Gwaun, the Severn, the Usk, the Wye, and very many more. Most of these are pre-Celtic words. Sometimes they are combined with a Celtic prefix like Aber—meaning 'the estuary of', or 'the mouth of', so we get Aberystwyth, or Aberdyfi, or Aberteifi (the old name for Cardigan town). So it is with some mountain names like Cadair Idris. We know that Cadair is the Welsh for a chair—the old round-backed chair which is alike in shape to the cirques formed by the former glaciers on the mountain side, but we do not know 'the meaning' of *Idris* and all we can say is that it occurs very frequently as a boy's name in this country and is found in Islamic lands like North Africa as well. It may be useful to end this short statement with a very brief list of Welsh words which occur very commonly in place-names and are at the same time descriptive in the main of geographical features.

Aber (estuary, mouth of)	Moel (Foel) (bare hill-top)
Afon (river)	Morfa (bog, fen, sea-marsh)
Banc (bank, hill, slope)	Mynydd (mountain)
Blaen (end, source, summit)	Nant (brook)
Bwlch (pass, gap)	Pant (hollow, valley)
Caer (gaer) (fort)	Penrhyn (promontory)
Cefn (ridge)	Plas (hall, mansion)
Craig (rock)	Pont (bridge)
Cwm (valley)	Porth (gateway, harbour)
Eglwys (church)	Rhos (moor, plain)
Garth (hill, enclosure)	Traeth (beach, shore)
Glyn (deep valley, glen)	Tref (town, homestead)
Llan (church, religious settlement)	Ynys (island, watermeadow)
Llyn (lake)	Ystrad (valley floor, strath)

Sources. Rhestr o Enwau Lleoedd—A Gazetteer of Welsh Place-names, Ed. Elwyn Davies: University of Wales Press, 1967: *A Glossary of Geographical Terms*, Ed. L. Dudley Stamp: London, 1961.

ONE DAY I'LL SING, ONE DAY I'LL DANCE FOR WALES

The International Eisteddfod is held each year at Llangollen. Choirs and teams of dancers come from many countries to compete, wearing their national costumes and joining together with enthusiasm. This Eisteddfod has become a symbol of goodwill and peace.

There are Guides and Scouts in nearly every country who also join together in international events and maintain links of friendship throughout the world.

In this photograph a Welsh team of Guide dancers, chosen from different parts of the Principality, take part in an International Festival wearing national dress which had been handed down in their families for generations, one being a wedding dress of an ancestress.

E. G. BOWEN

Some Welsh Women
of the Past

W ALES like other countries has had its distinguished men and women in the past, but so often the story of the great men seems to have overshadowed that of the great women. This is altogether unfair. In this book it behoves us to turn more particularly to the outstanding women of Wales in the past. Selection is not easy, but everyone would agree that we are on safe ground in beginning with the great Queen Elizabeth I, who together with her ancestors was particularly proud and very conscious of her Welsh descent. The Tudor family could trace its ancestry back to the native Princes of Wales and especially to those of Gwynedd. Queen Elizabeth's great- great-grandfather was Owain Tudor, himself a descendant of the Welsh princes whose home was in Penmynydd in Anglesey. He fell in love with Catherine of France, the widow of King Henry V, and one of their sons had married Margaret Beaufort, a descendant of John of Gaunt, who in turn became the mother of Henry VII. After the Battle of Bosworth in 1485, Henry ascended the English throne as the first monarch of the Tudor dynasty. Henry was, of course, Queen Elizabeth's grandfather and we know that he had been brought up in Pembroke Castle by a Welsh nurse and that he himself was almost certainly able to speak the Welsh language. On the field of battle at Bosworth he unfurled the Red Dragon of Wales; he called his eldest son Arthur, hoping that one day Britain would again have a King Arthur, as of old. This, however, was not to be, as Arthur died a very young man and the crown passed to Henry VIII and after him to his children, the most distinguished of whom was unquestionably Queen Elizabeth. She had the great advantage of living in spacious times, when the boundaries of human experience suddenly widen and the spirit of man leaps forward to possess and explore new domains. This was the Age of the Renaissance of Learning and the Reformation of the Church, the Age of the great seamen like Drake and Hawkins—the Age of the Armada and of William Shakespeare. Outside England it was the time when Erasmus and Luther taught, when Raphael and Michelangelo painted, when Columbus and Vespucci and Vasco da Gama founded new lands beyond the seas, an Age when the printing press and gunpowder were used for the first time. Men and women felt that a new world was opening up before them and indeed, some six years before the princess was born, Robert Thorne in Bristol had exlaimed that 'there was no sea unnavigable nor land unhabitable'. When Elizabeth grew up and became Queen she seems to have become the embodiment of all this—the living symbol of the New Age. Her childhood was not unhappy. She read widely and zealously in the Greek and Latin classics and we know that she was a fluent speaker in French, Italian, and, later, in Spanish, and that she also had good handwriting. Her knowledge of these foreign languages helped her greatly later on when she became Queen, for she was able to discuss with foreign ambassadors directly and so in secret with no interpreters present. In these circumstances she often got her own way. She was indeed an impressive figure, tall with reddish gold hair (she is wearing a wig unfortunately in our picture) and a somewhat olive complexion. Her accession to the throne was welcomed by almost universal rejoicing and she was determined from the start to govern herself

QUEEN ELIZABETH I

and mastered the art of government to the full. Like her father and grandfather before her, she had an uncanny intuition of when it was wise to take a risk, especially if the risk involved doing nothing at all in a crisis. She played her cards extremely well. On one occasion in 1577 she heard that certain Welsh ships from Pembrokeshire and Monmouthshire were about to set out on a pirating expedition against Spain led by Sir William Morgan. She immediately put a stop to this venture so as not to annoy the Spaniards. The culprit was, however, assured privately by the Queen that 'he was well thought of on account of this, both by her Majesty and their Lordships'. In this way was peace kept with Spain, without affronting these enterprising seamen upon whom reliance would have to be placed should the peace break down. As the late Professor Raleigh said, Queen Elizabeth had unlimited tact; 'she kept in with the police and did not fall out with the thieves'! Though she loved to steer the ship of state with her own hands and did it with consummate skill, yet she was not afraid to choose the ablest men in the land to serve her, but she was quick to resent any attempt of even the greatest of her favourites to dictate to her. This same determination not to give herself a master, no doubt explains why she never married, even with the great risk this involved of leaving the throne without an heir. Behind all this we can see the great determination, the innate ability, and the calculated shrewdness of the Welsh character. The great Queen was not unmindful of Wales and of all things Welsh. If we look at Bishop Morgan's great translation of the Bible into Welsh (issued in the same year as the Armada came) we see the Royal Arms displayed on the title-page. The Crown is supported by a Lion Rampant, on one side, and by the Red (or sometimes gold) Dragon Rampant of Wales on the other. The Welsh Dragon had been used as a supporter by all the Tudor monarchs, and it was James I, on his accession in 1603, who substituted the Unicorn for the Red Dragon on the Royal Arms, and unfortunately for Wales the Unicorn has remained there ever since. Queen Elizabeth was a remarkable, courageous, and gifted woman who dedicated herself to a life of service to her people. She could speak with force and emotion in public, coupled with a wonderful style, and choice of phrase, echoed in our own time by a man like Sir Winston Churchill. It is most interesting to compare their great speeches, rallying the people of these islands when threatened with imminent invasion. Churchill's peroration in 1940 is universally acclaimed a masterpiece: '. . . we shall not flag or fail, we shall go on to the end . . . we shall defend our island whatever the cost may be, we shall fight on the beaches, we shall fight on the landing grounds, we shall fight in the fields and in the streets, we shall fight in the hills, we shall never surrender', but Elizabeth in a similar situation in 1588, and lacking the resources on land, on the sea, and in the air, that Churchill possessed, was at once more realistic and more masculine: '. . . and think foul scorn that Palma or Spain, or any prince of Europe should dare to invade the borders of my realm'. Churchill envisaged the enemy as crossing our borders, but Elizabeth was not prepared to contemplate anything of the kind! She was able to keep this wonderful power of rallying the nation behind her to the very end, and we can give no better picture of her than she gives of herself in another speech to Parliament towards the close of her reign: 'Though God hath raised me high, yet I account the glory of my crown that I have reigned with your loves. . . . It is not my desire to live or reign longer than my life or reign shall be for your good. And though you have had, and may have, many mightier and wiser princes sitting in this seat, yet you never had, nor shall have, any that will love you better.'

We must now turn to a Welsh woman of a later age, one of equal beauty, tall, dignified with dark expressive eyes—one of the greatest actresses ever seen on the English stage. She was Mrs. Sarah Siddons, born the eldest of twelve children of Roger and Sarah Kemble, at the 'Shoulder of Mutton' public house in Brecon on 5 July 1755. Her parents were actors in a company that performed in a local theatre in Brecon and travelled around the Border towns of Wales. The house in which she was born is still to be seen, no longer a public house but a private house known as 'The Siddons', with a plaque over the doorway to commemorate the birthplace of the great actress. Sarah travelled around with her parents and was on the stage since the days of her youth. She had, however, a good education at Worcester and Wolverhampton. Then one day in 1772 a young actor named William Siddons joined this famous Brecon company and it was not long before he fell in love with Sarah Kemble. The Kemble family, however, disapproved of the match, and William was dismissed from the Company and Sarah went into domestic service with a family living in a remote part of Warwickshire. In the end love triumphed and the couple were married in Trinity Church, Coventry, on 26 November 1773. As Mrs. Siddons she played at Cheltenham, Bristol, and Bath, and her acting was such that many in the audience were moved to tears and others fainted and had to be carried out—so vivid were her representations. Soon she was invited by the great Garrick to appear in Drury Lane in London and was offered the magnificent salary of £5 a week. After some initial difficulties she reigned supreme in Drury Lane throughout the last quarter of the eighteenth and the beginning of the nineteenth centuries, receiving the praise and approval of the famous men of her day, including the poet Byron and the famous Dr. Johnson himself. She excelled in parts that required great dignity and emotion and probably played Lady Macbeth better than anyone has done before or since. She also scored immense praise for her portrayal of Desdemona, Rosalind, and Ophelia. After the days of her youth in Brecon she did not spend long periods in Wales again, but she did make occasional visits to her friend Mrs. Piozzi at Brynbela in the Vale of Clwyd and always maintained her affection for the Welsh countryside. The curious thing is that Mrs. Siddons is as much remembered for the great portraits that were painted of her by famous artists in her lifetime as she is for the greatness of her acting. She sat for almost all the great painters of the day, and Gainsborough's painting of her is one of his best and hangs in the National Gallery in London. The picture you see here is of Mrs. Siddons taking a leading part in a play and was painted by Sir Joshua Reynolds and is said to be a masterpiece of its kind. Mrs. Siddons was still acting at the end of George III's reign, but died in London shortly afterwards on 8 June 1831. She lies buried in Paddington, but like so many of our national heroes and famous men and women in all walks of life, she has a memorial in Westminster Abbey.

It is interesting to compare Sarah Siddons with another Welsh woman of an entirely different type, namely Elizabeth Davies of Bala who achieved fame as one of Florence Nightingale's assistants in the hospitals of Scutari and Balaclava in the Crimean War in the middle of the last century. She had the most romantic and adventurous career that any Welsh woman could obtain and had a long record of travel and adventure coupled with great fortitude long before she landed in Scutari. She is interesting in the way in which she is so very Welsh on the one hand, being a farmer's daughter from Welsh Wales and a faithful Calvinistic Methodist and Sunday School scholar, and yet so untypical, in that she literally roamed the world, suffered great hardships, and became involved in escapades which would have daunted most men even in her day.

She was born in the year 1789 at Pen-rhiw, a farm-house near Bala. Her father and mother were Mr. and Mrs. Dafydd

SARAH SIDDONS

ELIZABETH DAVIES

Cadwaladr (a real ancient Celtic name). She was therefore originally known as Beti Cadwaladr, or as is so usual in Welsh Wales known by a combination of her Christian name and that of the farm on which she lived. So she was known to her friends in Bala as Beti or Betsi Pen-rhiw. Her mother died when she was very young and she spent a lot of her youth in Bala with relatives. She grew up to be a strong healthy girl and was most often found playing with the boys, and performing the same feats of climbing and jumping as they did and often beating them at it. When she was ten years old she was presented with a Bible by the great Thomas Charles of Bala, her minister, for her faithfulness in attending the local Sunday School. She carried this Bible with her on her journeys across the world and treasured it greatly, arguing that it had protected her in many a crisis. In spite of this very orthodox background she was, nevertheless, very unconventional in other ways. Contrary to the ideas of her chapel in those days she loved dancing—it had the strongest attraction for her, and many times to the horror of Thomas Charles she distinguished herself on the dance floor. She was seized with a great desire to see the world and we hear of her at the age of fifteen escaping secretly by night from her home and journeying to Liverpool where she had relatives. She managed to get into domestic service with a rich family there, and travelled with them on the Continent at an early age. In Liverpool, too, she adopted the name Davies as the English people, according to her, could not pronounce the difficult word Cadwaladr. She was thereafter known as Elizabeth Davies. She left the service of this rich family and embarked herself on a seafaring career and went on voyages in sailing ships to places as far apart as the West Indies, Australia, Tasmania, China, India, Africa, and South America. As is to be expected such voyages were in her day hazardous in the extreme and the dangers great. She never lost her nerve in the greatest storms or in the most tempestuous seas. She is accredited on one occasion with lowering the sails single-handed in a crisis amidst a terrible storm and thereby saving the vessel, already filling with water, when the captain and the crew had panicked. When she was on land adventure seems to have followed adventure especially when she went into the jungle in search of wild flowers, in which she was very interested, and found lions and panthers as well. Yet she never forgot her Welsh background and sought out everyone who could speak Welsh wherever she roamed. She met some of the most distinguished missionaries of the day, including the great William Carey in India and John Davies in Tahiti, and even the still better known Reginald Heber (who wrote the well-known hymn which begins with the lines: 'From Greenland's icy mountains, From India's coral strand . . .'). When Beti met Bishop Heber in India she was most surprised that he asked her about Bala and Wales and about his friend of former years Thomas Charles. He proceeded to recite in Welsh part of an elegy to the great Thomas Charles and was astounded to learn that he was speaking to the daughter of Dafydd Cadwaladr who had written the poem. After a long life of adventure and travel in this way she ultimately returned to London to live with her sister, and decided at this late hour to go in for hospital nursing. She was accepted at Guy's Hospital and took to the work of administering to the sick with great devotion and earnestness.

One morning after breakfast in September 1854 she was reading *The Times* newspaper and came across the news of the Battle of Alma which had just been fought in the Crimea. The article told of the hundreds of English soldiers who were dying not only from wounds but from cholera and the intense cold. There was evidence, too, of a serious lack of organization in the military hospitals. Beti determined there and then to go out and assist. She just missed Florence Nightingale's first party with forty-six other nurses but joined the second. It should be remembered that this was the first time that women had gone as nurses to military field hospitals. The conditions at Scutari hospital were such that the authorities said that they could not accommodate women and that they must return to England. But Elizabeth insisted and was finally allowed to join the hospital staff at Scutari. The wounded had to be taken in ships, with their wounds unattended, across the Black Sea from the Crimea to this hospital and arrived there in a piteous state. Beti Davies determined to go across the Black Sea on her own responsibility and attend to the soldiers in the base hospital at Balaclava. She was one of the first eleven women to go over. She attended to the wounded and took out bandages from the stores and cut up linen without permission to deal with urgent cases. Her own quarters were unsanitary and deplorable. Her bedroom was rat infested and not even rainproof. She often woke up in the morning to find her bed soaked with rain and the rats sleeping on the bedclothes. Ultimately, she was in charge of the kitchens by day and tended the wounded by night, and when her health gave way she was forced to return to London. Many common soldiers and high-ranking officers came to the ship to wish her goodbye, and to thank her in person for saving their lives. Above all, Miss Davies was among the few, War Office officials and high-ranking military officers included, who could stand up to Florence Nightingale. This famous lady, in spite of the glamour that surrounds her name, was haughty and imperious in manner and found it difficult to work with others. Beti Cadwaladr went her own way—direct to the wounded soldiers' bedside and was prepared to deal with Miss Nightingale afterwards. Many letters bear testimony to Beti's courage and self-sacrifice in the Crimea, but unlike Mrs. Siddons she has no memorial in Westminster Abbey, or, indeed, any known grave in London, where she died in 1860. We can best end the story of this remarkable woman from Bala by quoting a tribute to her memory by one of her superior officers in the Crimea.

'Nothing that can be said would be more than is justly due to this faithfulest of Her Majesty's Nurses. This respectable and truly good woman who has sacrificed her health, almost life, for the good of her suffering countrymen.'

Sources. R. B. Wernham, *Elizabeth I*, Enc. Brit. 8. 362–5: J. E. Neale, *Queen Elizabeth*, London, 1934: L. C. B. Seaman, *Post-Victorian Britain, 1902–1951*, London, 1966: G. J. Thomas, *Sarah Siddons*, Hamdden Cyf. III. Rhif. 23, 1966: Meirion Jones, *Elizabeth Davies 1789–1860*, University of Wales Press, 1960.

HOSPITALITY

No one of this nation ever begs, for the houses of all are common to all; and they consider liberality and hospitality amongst the first virtues.

GIRALDUS CAMBRENSIS

MEDIEVAL WELSH RECIPE

If you would at all times be merry, eat saffron in meat or drink, and you will never be sad. But beware of eating too much, lest you should die of excessive joy.

THE PHYSICIANS OF MYDDFAI

FOLK DANCERS

YOUNG WEAVERS

WELSH HARPIST

SIABOD

Leonard Jackson. By courtesy of Country Quest

CAERNARFON CASTLE

66

THE THREE FEATHERS WITHIN A
PRINCELY CORONET

SAINT DAVID
AND THE
WELSH BANNER
BADGES AND
EMBLEMS

THE DRAGON SUPPORTER
OF HENRY VII

THE DRAGON SUPPORTER
OF QUEEN ELIZABETH

With lifted hand St. David blessed the bees

RETOLD BY HILDA LLYWELYN WILLIAMS

ST. DAVID

ALTHOUGH it has not yet been possible to establish the exact dates of St. David's birth and death, it is reasonable to deduce that he lived during the second half of the fifth century and the first half of the sixth century. There are no available contemporary references to St. David, but mention is made of him in early church records, the earliest being found in the *Catalogue of the Saints of Ireland*—A.D. 730. Corroborative references occur in other church records, from Brittany and from St. David's itself, but the first biography proper was written in 1090 by Rhygyfarch, son of Bishop Sulien of St. David's. It is to this life of St. David that we owe most of what is known of the Patron Saint of Wales. The author claims that he has drawn on very old manuscripts, some in the hand of the Saint himself, for the substance of this biography. In this short chapter, it is not proposed to try to sift the probable from the improbable, but, instead, to cover briefly the life of St. David as set out by Rhygyfarch, recounting only the best known of the miracles associated with, or attributed to, the Saint.

Now, it happened that St. Patrick, during his wanderings in what is now west Wales, came upon a valley, Glyn Rhosyn, in the extreme west of Pembrokeshire. He was so attracted by it that he decided to settle there and make it the centre of his missionary work. Unknown to him, however, he had set himself work, and had chosen a site destined for another. This was revealed to him by an angel, who disclosed that from Glyn Rhosyn, one, who would not be born until thirty years had passed, would do great things in the name of God. St. Patrick was rebelliously angry at first, but relented when the angel bent the mountains and smoothed the sea and showed him the whole of the isle of Ireland, saying, 'Exult, Patrick, for thou shalt be the apostle of the whole of that island which thou seest.' St. Patrick, thereupon, after making all preparations, set sail for Ireland. At the appointed time, and in fulfilment of the angel's forecast, David was born. His mother was Non, a beautiful nun, and his father Sant, son of King Ceredig. He was baptized by Aelfyw, Bishop of Munster, in a spring of pure water which miraculously appeared for the ceremony. The infant was held for immersion by a monk, who had from birth neither eyes nor nose, and, sensing the holiness of his charge, sprinkled his own face with the water, and immediately his countenance was made whole.

David spent his early life at Hen Fynyw, and grew into a young man full of virtue and grace. After being received into priesthood, he left to study under the scribe Paulinus, disciple of St. Germanus. Sometime towards the end of his stay, his master became blind, and asked each of his disciples in turn to examine his eyes. Obtaining relief from none, he turned to David, who, forbidden by modesty to look upon his master's countenance, touched and blessed his eyes, at once restoring their sight, and dispelling all pain.

68

Not long after this, David set out on mission work throughout Britain, and, among his other works, he founded and established some twelve monasteries, among them Glastonbury, Repton, Leominster, Raglan, and Llangyfelach. His wanderings in time brought him back to Hen Fynyw, and thence, accompanied by his disciples, he came upon Glyn Rhosyn, forsaken in his favour many years before by St. Patrick. Here, despite the hostility of the local chieftain Bwya, and the malicious temptings of Bwya's wife, he and his disciples laboured and toiled, and built a noble monastery. St. David imposed upon himself and on the brethren a life of extreme austerity: all day they worked with hand and foot, using only those tools which were necessary, and scorning everything that might ease their labours. Here, nothing was 'thine' or 'mine': everything was common; each in turn was the other's ox to pull the plough, and everyone, avoiding conversation, indulged in prayer and meditation. Meals were of the simplest—bread, and herbs, and water—and even of this fare, excess was forbidden lest it led to wantonness. St. David decreed and got implicit obedience, and himself was tireless in caring for the brethren, the needy, orphans, widows, and, indeed, everyone in need of succour and of hospitality. Entry into the monastic order was rigorous and difficult. Yet, such was its fame that kings and princes, discarding wealth and authority, chose to live and serve in complete obedience to St. David. One such was Constantine, king of the Cornishmen, who in time, and by faithful service, himself founded a monastery.

Among David's disciples was Modomnoc, who after his training left for mission work in Ireland. One of his special duties had been the care of the beehives, and a whole multitude of bees followed and settled on his ship. Distressed lest it should appear that he was denuding his former brethren, he returned to the monastery accompanied by the bees. He sought the holy father's presence and the bees returned to their former homes. St. David blessed him for his humility and Modomnoc again set sail. Once again the bees followed and once more he returned to David. His third attempt to sail ended in the same way, and this time David, after blessing the bees, allowed Modomnoc to take them with him to settle in a country where no bees had thrived before.

There came a time when David, at the direction of an angel, travelled abroad, receiving the gift of tongues to make his journeyings the easier. Accompanied by Eiludd and Teilo, he arrived at Jerusalem, where he was made Bishop by the Patriarch, and received from him four gifts. Some time after the return home of the Bishop David, a synod of all the bishops of Britannia was called at Llanddewibrefi. There came also a multitude of people, among them kings and princes and abbots; so many, indeed, that it became impossible for one voice to address them all. The purpose of the synod was urgent: heresy was making poisonous progress in the land and someone must be found capable of destroying that heresy in the hearts of everyone present. A tower of garments was therefore made, and it was agreed that he who could reach the ear of all should become chief bishop in all Britain. After all in turn had failed, Paulinus, noticing that his former disciple was not present, suggested that David, recently made Bishop by the Patriarch, should be invited.

Urgent messages were sent, but each time David in his modesty refused. At last he was persuaded to appear at the synod. Rejecting the pile of garments, he stood on a handkerchief spread on the ground. As he preached, a snow-white pigeon from Heaven remained on his shoulder and the ground rose into a hillock beneath his feet. His voice reached the furthermost and his argument dispelled every doubt. Blessed and extolled by all, he was declared Archbishop, and his monastery the chief in the whole of the land.

And so, simple yet powerful, modest yet unafraid, St. David lived a long life of service gladly given to God. He died on a day foretold to him, March the First, a day preserved to his memory in every Welsh heart.

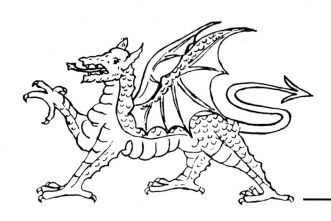

E. J. JONES

The Red Dragon

KING EDWARD VII granted to his son, afterwards King George, then Prince of Wales, and to his successors, an extra badge, which was described thus:

On a green mound a red dragon with elevated wings passant thereon, and for a difference a silver label of three points.

The other badge was the three ostrich feathers within a princely coronet and the motto *Ich Dien* within a scroll.

The Welsh dragon appears to have been used before the time of heraldry; as early as 1155 reference was made to the dragon as a crest borne by King Arthur.

During the Middle Ages people showed great interest in coats of arms, and when they were granted certain devices by the king or a prince it was natural for them to attribute their own arms to some far-off ancestor, although there was frequently no justification for assuming that they bore these arms. Welsh people were very proud of their descent from the early princes and kings, and of these we must mention Cadwallon, King of Gwynedd (north Wales) (5th cent.). This Cadwallon was believed to have borne the red dragon, and in the Middle Ages Welshmen often referred to the red dragon of Cadwallon. King Arthur's father, Uthr Pendragon, was thought to have borne on his yellow shield two green dragons standing back to back and wearing red crowns.

It was a compliment to be called a dragon (Welsh *draig*) by the Welsh poets, and thus the dragon was a popular device. Owain Glyndŵr, in 1401, had a standard of a golden dragon on a white field. We learn also, from Glyndŵr's *Great Seal*, as Prince of Wales, that he bore as his crest a *dragon (or wyvern) gules*. (Gules means red.) Glyndŵr's shield did not bear the dragon, but four rampant lions. The shield is described heraldically thus: *Quarterly or and gules, four lions rampant counter-changed*, i.e. the shield is divided into four parts and coloured yellow and red. In the yellow quarters are red rampant lions, and in the red quarters are golden lions.

We often see flags flown with this design as the Welsh flag. Sometimes, however, the lions are shown walking, not climbing, and these arms are believed to have been those of Llywelyn ab Iorwerth, Prince of Wales, who died in 1240.

When Henry Tudor became King of England he showed a keen interest in Welsh heraldry. He used as livery colours green and white, and on these colours his retainers had the red dragon painted. Henry VII also used a dragon as a supporter for his shield. (The supporters of the Royal Arms today are the lion and the unicorn.) The lower part of Henry VII's dragon was gold in colour and the upper part was red. Queen Elizabeth had a similar dragon as supporter, but the red was of darker shade, and might be called ruddy in colour. According to Welsh tradition the Welsh dragon was ruddy in colour.

Thus Welshmen recall the livery colours of Henry VII when they fly a green and white flag and the red dragon. Some battalions prefer to have white flags with a red dragon walking (as it were) on a green mound. The quartered flag of gold and red, with lions walking or climbing (rampant) is also favoured. This reminds us of the arms of Glyndŵr and of Llywelyn ab Iorwerth.

We frequently find also the words *Y ddraig goch ddyry gychwyn* used as a Welsh motto. The meaning of this sentence is best conveyed thus: 'The red dragon is our incentive.' (This is not a literal translation.)

★ ★ ★

The following facts may prove of interest:

When Edward of Woodstock fought the French at the battle of Crecy, he had a strong body of Welsh archers, who were dressed in green and white. The prince unfurled a flag on which was a red dragon. This prince's sword, which is still in Canterbury Cathedral, has dragons worked round the handle.

When Henry VII entered London after the battle of Bosworth, he went to St. Paul's Cathedral, where he offered up a standard of white and green, on which was a red dragon.

The Wyvern. On Glyndŵr's crest as it appears on his helmet (on his Great Seal) there is a red dragon or wyvern. A wyvern is a winged dragon with front legs only. We cannot see the hind legs, but we may assume that this crest is actually a dragon.

THE SHIELD
OF PEACE
OF THE
BLACK PRINCE

The Three Feathers

THE three Ostrich Feathers are now familiar to us as one of the badges of the Prince of Wales, and for this reason they are regarded with special interest by Welshmen. The history of these feathers as a badge is not fully known generally. Some writers have maintained that the Ostrich Feathers were adopted by the Black Prince after the capture of John, King of Bohemia, at the battle of Crecy; but there is no proof of this. The first mention of the feather as a badge occurs in the year 1370 when it was used by Queen Philippa. The Black Prince refers to badges of Ostrich Feathers in his will (1376), where he directs that at his funeral the Ostrich Feathers be carried on shields as emblems of peace, and his quartered arms of France and England as signs of war. But these feathers were single and not grouped in threes. Subsequently, many royal princes bore the Ostrich Feather as a badge, and each one modified the feather by some distinctive colours. Edward V as Prince of Wales displayed *an ostrich feather supported by a lion and having the motto ich dien*, 'I Serve', and Arthur Tudor, as Prince of Wales, had the same ostrich feather and motto, but it was *supported by a dragon*.

It was not until the time of the Stuarts that the *Three Ostrich Feathers grouped within the circlet of a prince's coronet* was recognized as the Prince's badge.

BADGE OF ARTHUR TUDOR AS PRINCE OF WALES

BADGE OF EDWARD V AS PRINCE OF WALES

The Leek and the Daffodil

THE leek and the daffodil, as national emblems, are also interesting. Henry V was proud of being Welsh and thus the reference to the leek in Shakespeare's Henry V is significant.

Even in the battle of Crecy the Welsh wore leeks as an honourable badge of service, and thus Fluellen (Llywelyn) felt deeply insulted when the leek was despised by Pistol on St. David's Day.

Why was the leek worn especially on St. David's Day?

St. David is the patron saint of Wales, and the leek was associated with him. The poet Michael Drayton, who wrote during the same time as Shakespeare, and who was interested in Welsh tales, said:

> *That reverend British saint, in zealous ages past*
> *To contemplation lived, and did so truly fast,*
> *As he did only drink what crystal Hodney yields*
> *And fed upon the leeks he gathered in the fields.*
> *In memory of whom, in each revolving year*
> *The Welshmen on his day that sacred herbe do wear.*

According to another tradition the Welsh wore the leek when fighting against the Saxons at the battle of Heathfield (A.D. 633).

The leek was very popular in Tudor times, and we learn from Princess Mary's Privy Purse Expenses that presents were given by her to the Yeomen of the Guard on St. David's Day, when she was presented with a leek. On this day, too, the King and members of the royal family gave money presents to Welsh harpists who sang at Court.

The Welsh name of the daffodil is *Cenhinen Pedr* (Peter's Leek) and *Cenhinen Fawrth* (March Leek). People were therefore led to believe that this flower was the national emblem. Evidence, however, definitely favours the adoption of the leek; but the beautiful daffodil has come to stay, and it will be henceforth accepted, along with the leek.

The Welsh National Anthem

HEN WLAD FY NHADAU

Mae hen wlad fy nhadau yn annwyl i mi,
Gwlad beirdd a chantorion, enwogion o fri;
Ei gwrol ryfelwyr, gwladgarwyr tra mad,
Dros ryddid collasant eu gwaed.
Gwlad! Gwlad! pleidiol wyf i'm Gwlad;
Tra môr yn fur i'r bur hoff bau,
O, bydded i'r hen iaith barhau!

THE LAND OF MY FATHERS

Old land of my fathers, so dear unto me,
Famed land of the Minstrel, fair home of the free;
Thy warriors who wielded, undaunted, thy sword,
For Freedom their life-blood have poured.
Wales! Wales! true am I to Wales;
While seas surge 'round, we raise the sound,
O live ye loved land evermore!

Stories of the Red Dragon

THE LEGEND OF UTHR PENDRAGON

OF all legendary creatures the dragon is one of the most ancient. Many centuries ago this fabulous monster crawled and wriggled and flew its way all over Europe and Asia, and many kings and princes have followed the dragon standard into battle.

There is an old legend which tells how the father of King Arthur, Uthr Pendragon, saw a flaming dragon in the sky, foretelling that he would be king. When this prophecy was fulfilled Uthr ordered two dragon standards to be made, one to be dedicated in Winchester Cathedral, the other to be borne before him into battle. His son King Arthur is one of the legendary heroes of Wales and it is said that this story explains how the Red Dragon became our national emblem.

MERLIN'S FIRST PROPHECY

KING VORTIGERN, in fear of his enemies, decided to build a strong castle in the kingdom of Gwynedd. Artificers and the craftsmen set to work in a wild region near the summit of Snowdon. When each night the new-made walls collapsed, wise men advised breaking the spell by sprinkling the site with the blood of a fatherless child.

Away in Carmarthen the King's messengers discovered Merlin, a boy of lost parentage. He laughed when they were about to put him to death, saying it would not help their work. Then his prophecies stayed their hand for all time. Commanding them to dig deep below the fallen walls, he foretold the discovery of a pond, and deeper still a strange sight in two great hollow stones.

'What means this?' exclaimed King Vortigern as, horrified, the workmen fell back at the sight of two dragons.

Roused, the two dragons who had been sleeping started to fight. 'Look,' Merlin said, 'the white dragon of the Saxon and the red dragon of the Celt; even so will two nations fight.'

'Which will lose?' King Vortigern cried; but Merlin only smiled that mysterious smile of a wizard, and the two dragons disappeared in the strange mountain mist.

THE TWO DRAGONS

THERE is a curious mark on one of the Welsh mountains. It looks like an old quarry now, but it marks the spot where Y Ddraig Goch (The Red Dragon) and the White Dragon fought their last battle.

It happened that the Red Dragon and the White Dragon were walking round the mountain in opposite directions. They never saw each other until their noses met. 'What are you doing crawling round my mountain?' shouted the White Dragon. 'Your mountain!' roared the Red Dragon, 'Never!' 'It has always been mine, and will be for ever', hissed the White Dragon. 'It has never been yours,' screamed the Red Dragon, 'and it never will be.' They then blew out fire and smoke so that the earth was scorched all around them.

Now the White Dragon was beautiful, with pink on his ears and golden eyes; but the Red Dragon was glorious indeed, glowing red, with eyes like rubies and a tail twisted like a wicked serpent.

'Ha!' snarled the White Dragon, 'I'll teach you to walk on my mountain, for I am the Sais Dragon and all the land is mine. Come on and fight.' 'Hu Oui,' snorted the Red Dragon, 'I am Y Ddraig Goch, Dragon of the Cymry, and I will fight until this land is free and all is for Cymry once more.' And so they fought for many years, and the noise was like the roaring of many waters and their breath filled the valleys like mist. They fought until the mountain crumbled and the mark you see was the last feeble scratching of the White Dragon as it lay down and died. The mountain belongs to the sons of Cymry to this day and our Welsh flag and crest commemorate for ever the victory of Y Ddraig Goch.

Royal Badge of Wales

On Wednesday, 11 March 1953, Her Majesty the Queen was pleased, by and with the advice of her Privy Council, to order that for the greater honour and distinction of Wales the Royal Badge of Wales be augmented as follows: 'Within a circular band argent fimbriated *or* bearing the motto Y DDRAIG GOCH DDYRY CYCHWYN in letters *vert*, and ensigned with a representation of the Crown proper, an escutcheon perfesse argent and vert and thereon a Red Dragon passant.'

74

RETOLD BY MARY HALE PUCKLE AND
HETHER KAY

LEGENDS
AND
FOLK TALES
OF WALES

STORIES FROM HISTORY

B. P.

THE LADY OF THE LAKE

IN the Black Mountains there is a lonely lake called Llyn-y-Fan Fach. In olden times there lived here a widow with one son, whose name was Gwyn. Every day Gwyn drove his cattle to graze by the lake, and one day he was amazed to see a beautiful lady standing in the clear water. As he gazed spellbound, he unconsciously held out the hard baked barley bread that his mother had made for him. The lady glided towards him, shook her head, and said,

Cras dy fara   'Oh thou of the crimped bread
Nid hawdd fy nala   It is not easy to catch me',

and she dived out of sight. Next day Gwyn was there again and this time he took some unbaked dough. Towards evening the lady appeared but again she shook her head, saying,

Llaith dy fara,   'Oh thou of the moist bread
Ti ni fynna   I will not have thee'.

The third day his mother gave him some half-baked bread and to his joy the lovely lady took the gift and allowed him to lead her to dry land. 'I love you', he cried, 'more than all the world. Will you be my wife?' At first she would not consent, but at last she promised, on one condition, that if he should give her three blows without cause she would leave him for ever.

Her father gave her as a dowry as many sheep, cattle, goats, swine, and horses as she could count without drawing breath, and as she counted they came up out of the Lake and stood beside her on the bank. So Gwyn and the Lady of the Lake were married. She called herself Nelfach, and for many years they lived happily and had three sons.

One day they were invited to a wedding. The way was long and Nelfach grew weary and vowed she could go no farther. 'Go and catch a horse then and we will ride', said Gwyn, and he flicked her playfully with the gloves he was carrying. Instantly she turned and looked at him; 'That is the first causeless blow', she said.

Years afterwards they went together to a christening. All was joy and merriment, but Nelfach suddenly burst into tears. Gwyn tapped her on the shoulder. 'Why do you weep?' he asked. 'I weep', she said, 'because of all that may befall this babe, so weak and frail he is. And husband,' she added, 'you have dealt me the second causeless blow.' Poor Gwyn was now on his guard night and day, for he knew his heart would break if she left him.

Some years later the babe died, and Gwyn and Nelfach were bidden to the funeral. In the midst of all the mourning and grief, Nelfach laughed merrily. Her husband was shocked and touched her saying, 'Hush, why do you laugh?' 'I laugh', she said, 'because this poor babe is at last happy and free from pain. Now I must say Farewell, for you have struck me the third time.'

As she ran towards the Lake, all her sheep and cattle followed her, and together they disappeared beneath the waters. All that was left was the furrow made by the plough which the oxen drew after them into the Lake, and this remains to this day.

Gwyn was heartbroken and put an end to his misery by plunging into the depths of the Lake. Their sons spent their days wandering up and down in the hopes of seeing their mother once more.

One day Nelfach appeared to them and led them to a place still called Physician's Dingle, where she taught them the healing powers of all the plants and herbs that grew there. 'Your part on earth', she told them, 'is to relieve the pain and misery of mankind.' From her they learnt the art of healing and became skilful physicians in the land.

The Lord of Llandovery gave them land and privileges at Myddfai and the fame of the 'Physicians of Myddfai' spread over the whole of Wales and continued for many centuries among their descendants.

THE LEGEND OF THE THREE RIVERS

HIGH up on the slopes of Plinlimon lived three sisters, Wye, Severn, and Rheidol. All day they played and splashed in the clear water that bubbled out of the mountain side, or lay on the short turf looking out towards the far distance; and here on a clear day they could see the sea sparkling blue and silver in the sunshine. When the wind blew from the west it brought with it the scent of salt and seaweed mingling with the heather and peat of the mountains, and the sisters were filled with a longing to go out into the world, to take their pure spring water down to the parched valleys below, and especially they longed to find the way that led to the sea.

One day they decided that the following morning they would get up early and set off together on their quest. Wye was the first to awaken. She dressed herself carefully and in the grey dawn slipped quietly into the valley. All day she wandered slowly through the lovely countryside and the little mountain stream spread out behind her like a train, getting wider and wider as she went, and as there was no need for her to hurry she was still looking fresh and fair when at last she reached the sea.

A little later Severn awoke, and when she saw that Wye had already gone she hurried off as quickly as she could. 'I will soon catch her up', she said, but when she reached the valley, in her haste she took the wrong turning and went many miles out of her way before she at last met her sister at the entrance to the sea.

The sun was high in the sky when Rheidol sat up and found that she was alone. In a panic she rushed down the mountain side, going she knew not where, and unknowingly she took the shortest way and before long tumbled headlong into the sea, but she never saw her sisters again.

And because the Wye got up early and had no need to hurry she is the most beautiful river in Wales, while the Severn, who lost her way, is the longest, and the little Rheidol who overslept is Wales's shortest river.

PENNARD CASTLE

PENNARD CASTLE in Gower now lies desolate and lost in the sandhills, but once it was a mighty fortress, the stronghold of a great warrior. For his bravery and skill in war he was rewarded with the hand of the Chief's daughter in marriage and on the eve of the wedding the castle echoed with the sounds of feasting and revelry.

At midnight a sentry, keeping guard on the castle walls, heard faint music and looking down he saw a strange sight. There on the greensward, dancing in the moonlight to the music of many tiny harps, was a troop of fairies. With fear in his heart he ran to the banqueting hall to tell his master what he had seen. Now the Lord of the Castle was full of good wine and he ordered his soldiers to drive the fairies away. 'Have a care,' said one of the guests, 'for he who attacks a fairy is for ever doomed.' 'What care I,' answered the Chieftain, 'I fear neither man nor spirit', and he rushed from the hall to the moonlit spot brandishing his sword and thrusting this way and that in a vain effort to drive out the intruders. The guests cowering terror-stricken in the background heard the dreaded voice pronounce their doom. 'He who spoils the fairy dance shall himself be spoiled of all he possesses.'

The words had scarcely been spoken when a great wind arose carrying with it a whirling cloud of sand. Fiercer and fiercer raged the storm and when the day dawned the castle lay buried. The fairies had had their revenge and a mountain of sand was removed from Ireland that night.

EDNYFED FYCHAN'S HARP

EDNYFED FYCHAN was Commander-in-Chief to Llywelyn ab Iorwerth, Prince of all Wales. He was a mighty man of valour, but when the call came for him to go to the Crusades he was bitterly grieved to leave his wife, Gwenllian, whom he loved deeply. She was the daughter of Rhys, Prince of South Wales. Before leaving, her husband composed a lament called 'Ednyfed Fychan's Farewell', which he played for her on his harp.

The Crusades over, Gwenllian, left with no news, was at last persuaded that Ednyfed was gone for always, that he was dead. Only with this realization did she at last agree to marry one who had urged and begged that she would do so for a long time.

The night before the wedding, a great feast was held at Llys Euryn. When all the guests were assembled, a beggar came quietly into the hall; he stood spellbound, watching, then he asked if he could borrow a harp which was formerly there. Sadly the strains of 'Ednyfed's Lament' sounded through the hall. The bride, white to the lips, rose and moved slowly down the great room as one in a dream, till she stood by the ragged Crusader harpist. Looking up into his eyes she knew him to be her husband. Then the hall rang with the deafening clamour of those gathered at the banquet who hailed their returning Chieftain.

THE LAMBS OF MELANGELL

LONG ago in the year 604, Brochwel, the Prince of Powys, was hunting in a place called Pennant in the Land of Wales. Suddenly his hounds started in full cry after a hare which dashed into a dense thicket. Following his hounds the Prince came to a clearing in the wood where, to his astonishment, he saw a beautiful maiden on her knees praying below a Cross which had been made of silver birch branches. The hare was quietly sitting on the folds of her long dress facing the hounds boldly. The Prince urged on his hounds to catch the hare, but howling they backed fearfully away, then turning they rushed off into the undergrowth and were lost to sight.

The maiden rose to her feet. 'Who are you?' asked the Prince in wonder at the behaviour of his hounds, 'and what does this mean?'

'I am Melangell, the daughter of a King of Ireland,' she answered, 'and because my father wanted me to marry one of his Chiefs, I fled from my country and, God guiding me, came to this lonely place where for fifteen years I have served God in solitude.'

The Prince was amazed at the strength of her faith. 'Melangell,' he said, 'because God has given you the power to protect the weak from the fury of the strong, so that even a little hare finds safety in your presence, I here and now give you these my lands for the service of God, to be a perpetual sanctuary to all—men, women, and all other living things who flee hither to seek your protection. Let no Prince or Chieftain be so rash towards God as to attempt to drive them forth.'

Melangell passed the rest of her days in this lonely place and many were the miracles she wrought for those who sought her protection. The little wild hares were her special friends, and that is why they are called Melangell's Lambs.

The Legend of Llyn Safaddan

The winter wind blew thinly in the reeds
Beside Safaddan Lake. Three racing steeds,
Tuned to their riders' mood, grew tensely still,
Trembling like echoes driven from hill to hill.
A vagrant mist came by, and seemed to rest
Where wild fowl crowded on the water's breast.

Then Milo spake. 'My lands and thine, O Payn—
Guarded by mountains, rich with sun and rain!
How good to be a Norman!' And he turned
Sharply, and smiling, but with eyes that burned.
''Tis mad Welsh fancy, Gruffydd, makes you hold
These lands are rightly yours! And since 'tis told
That birds of Lake Safaddan sing to own
Their rightful ruler, and for him alone—
And since you doubt the justice of the King,
I will make trial now, and bid them sing . . .
O Birds of Lake Safaddan, rise and claim
The mighty lord who rules in Henry's name!'
. . . His ringing challenge rose, and fell and brake
Where tranquil wings lay mirrored in the lake.

Then Payn dismounted at the water's edge.
'I hold my overlordship as a pledge

To serve the King: Therefore, ye silent throng,
I charge you by his power to raise your song!'
. . . The echoes jangled in the westering ray
With mockery at themselves, and died away.
So Gruffydd came. He came grave-eyed with truth,
One whose lost heritage had touched his youth.
And by the water-side he knelt in prayer,
As was his wont for battle; and the air
Heard and was still. . . . But suddenly he rose
And stretched his arms towards the mountain snows,
The dales, the little rills that laughed in flood—
Land of his fathers, yearning in his blood.
And all the hiraeth trembled in his voice,
Bidding the birds arise and sing their choice. . . .

Then shook the waters with a rush of wings—
Burst into music as a harp that sings . . .
A mighty sound from wheeling shades and gleams,
Surging with valorous faith, yet soft with dreams,
Voice of a freedom none shall ever break,
Proclaimed for Gruffydd by Safaddan Lake . . .
And shamed usurpers mused upon the wrong
That left a Cymric prince no crown but Song.

MELFIN JONES

Note.—In olden Wales it was said that the Birds of Llangorse Lake, Breconshire, knew who was the rightful prince of the district, and would sing for him at his bidding. This story is set in the time of King Henry the Second.

THE CHILDREN OF RHYS DDWFN

WHEN the thick white mists come in from the sea, the people of Cardigan look at each other and say, 'The Children of Rhys Ddwfn will be doing their marketing today.' Far out in Cardigan Bay lie the Ynysoedd Mulfrain (Cormorant Isles), invisible except to those who have eaten a certain herb found only on a small patch of ground near Cemmaes. Here the children of Rhys Ddwfn have lived for many centuries; they come to the mainland to buy corn for their bread, but no mortal eye has ever seen them. How they come or whence they go is a secret which only the sea knows.

GEESE

WOGAN AND THE DRAGON

IN a village near Haverfordwest, this story has been handed down from the Middle Ages. In those far-away days there lived here a dragon of great ferocity. Now a dragon is never a nice neighbour, but this one was worse than them all for it could, at will, render itself invisible, and all the people went in terror of their lives. It feared no one except a certain magician who had cast a spell over it so that the dragon knew that it would die if ever seen by human eye.

Confident of its powers of invisibility, the dragon would stalk through the village, shouting out in a harsh, croaking voice, 'Who gan zee me? Who gan zee me?' and devouring horses and cattle as if they were so many lollipops. Sometimes in desperation some brave spirits would conceal themselves in the bushes, hoping to catch a glimpse of the monster, but none of them ever returned home.

At last one of the villagers thought of a plan. With the help of his friends he concealed a large empty barrel in the wood near the place where the dragon lived. Hiding inside the barrel and peeping through the bung-hole he waited. Soon he heard the dragon plunging through the undergrowth bawling out at the top of his voice, 'Who gan zee me? Who gan zee me?' and being by this time full of arrogance and self-confidence, it had not troubled to make itself invisible.

The hidden watcher held his breath, then, as the dragon came in sight, he shouted with all his might, 'I can see thee, I can see thee.' The dragon stopped, gave out a hideous yell and blew up in a cloud of smoke.

The hero of the barrel was honoured with the title 'Who gan zee me', later shortened to 'Whogan', and to this day his descendants, now called 'Wogan', are to be found in the district.

THE LEGEND OF LLYN TEGID

ONCE upon a time there was no lake at Bala; instead there stretched a fertile valley and in it a town of stately palaces and beautiful gardens.

In the finest of these palaces there lived a wicked prince, so cruel and unjust that he was feared and hated by all. It was said that he feared neither God nor man, nor did he heed the warning voices which came to him, borne on the breeze, as he walked in his gardens. 'Vengeance will come,' whispered the voices, and he laughed at them and went on his wicked way and flourished exceedingly.

To celebrate the birth of his heir he prepared a sumptuous feast, to which kings and queens, princes and princesses, lords and ladies, from far and wide were invited. The richness of the food and wine and the splendour of the surroundings were such as had never been seen before, and through it all sounded the sweet music of the harp.

Now it happened that the harpist was an old man, and growing weary he withdrew to a quiet corner to rest. Suddenly he heard a voice saying softly, 'Vengeance will come', and looking up he saw a tiny bird flying above his head, beckoning to him to follow. Some unseen power compelled him to go, and laying down his harp he crept out into the night. The little bird led him to the top of a mountain. Here the old man lay down, and being tired out he fell into a deep sleep.

When he awakened it was morning. Stretched out before him was the valley full of water, underneath which lay the palace with all its splendour, lost for ever, and floating towards him on the smooth clear surface of the lake was his beloved harp.

80

THE GIRDLE OF TRUTH

'A CHAIN like gold, made like a dog's head, the teeth stretching outward.' So did Giraldus Cambrensis in the year 1188 describe this wonderful girdle, long preserved at Brecon.

The girdle was given by King Brychan to his eldest son, Cynog, when the latter was baptized by St. Gastayn. It possessed an extraordinary virtue inasmuch as when it was laid before him, no man dared swear falsely.

PRINCE BRYCHAN

LONG ago a boy sat with his tutor by the River Usk, near Brecon, watching the wild creatures and listening to the bees in a hollow beech tree.

Presently a wild boar came out of the wood, and following it a stag. For some moments they stood, the boar on the bank, the stag behind it knee-deep in the river, and a silver fish could be seen swimming under the stag. The boy watched, entranced, then, seeing the look on his tutor's face, he whispered, 'What does it mean?'

'It means for thee', said the tutor, 'a long and happy life, with riches as abundant as the golden honey in yonder tree.' He looked down into the boy's wondering eyes, and added, 'May the Grace of God remain with thee here and hereafter.' This boy was Prince Brychan, son of Prince Anlae.

THE WELL OF SAINT WINIFRED

HOLYWELL in Flintshire takes its name from the Well of Saint Winifred. Here in olden days pilgrims came from far and wide to wash in the miraculous waters and many were cured.

Saint Winifred lived early in the seventh century. Many sought her hand in marriage, amongst them a chieftain named Caradog, but she, having renounced the world and taken vows of chastity, refused him, and, when he would have taken her by force, fled to the hills. Determined to win, Caradog pursued her, but, in spite of all his threats, she remained faithful to her vows. Goaded to fury, the chieftain drew his sword and slashed off her head. His followers, watching the grim deed, saw him fall dead and the earth open and swallow him up. The severed head bounded down the hill and on the spot where it came to rest a well of pure water sprang up. The church was founded by Saint Beuno, uncle of Winifred, and the Saint himself took up the head and, as he prayed, it was united to the body and life was restored, nor could any mark be seen, save that of a slender white line round the neck.

St. Winifred lived for many years and having taken the veil died as Abbess of Gwytherin.

A TRIAD OF THE ISLE OF BRITAIN (Ancient History)

The three principal cities of the Isle of Britain:

Caer Llion upon Wysg in Cymru   = Caer Lleon upon Usk in Cambria
Caer Llundain in Lloegr   = London in Loegria
Caer Evrawg in Deifr and Brynaich = York in Deira and Bernicia.

BRANWEN THE BEAUTIFUL

From The Mabinogion

BUILT on a big crag of rock high above a plain towers Harlech Castle looking north to Snowdon and west across the Irish Sea. Legend says that Branwen's Tower stood here 1,000 years before Edward I built Harlech Castle. Here lived Brân the Blessed, King of Britain, and his sister Branwen, the fairest maid in all the land. To Harlech, Matholwch, King of Ireland, sailed and persuading Brân to agree he married Branwen at Aberffraw in Anglesey amid great festivities. A bitter quarrel arose, however, with Efnysien, Branwen's half-brother, and when the Irish King sailed away to the Isle of Saints with his bride Matholwch's anger soon turned on her. After their little son Gwern was born the king deposed her and ordered her to be cook in his palace.

Lonely and sad was Branwen. At last she reared a starling and tied a letter to its wing. The bird, it is said, flew to Brân and perching on his shoulder it flapped its wings till the letter was seen.

Furious at the fate of his sister, Brân embarked for Ireland with all his warriors. He went to his death for in the terrible fighting which followed they were nearly all killed. Seven escaped and came sadly home bringing Branwen and the King's head—by his wish—to rest seven years at Harlech, then to be set at White Mount in the City of Lud (Tower Hill, London).

Branwen cried as they landed in Anglesey: 'Woe is me that I was ever born, for two islands have been destroyed because of me.'

ST. ELIAN'S WELL

HOW Saint Elian's Well came to be changed from a holy wishing-well into a cursing well is for ever a mystery.

We cannot blame the Saint. He, feeling thirsty, knelt down and prayed for water. The well gushed out at his feet and he blessed it and went on his way.

Some years later it became one of the most dreaded spots in Wales. One day a man would be feeling healthy and happy, the next he would be so sick and sorry and weighed down by misfortune that life became a burden. Sooner or later it would reach his ears that his name, written on a piece of paper by an unknown enemy, had been given to the keeper of the well, who in return for a certain sum of money had recited the special curse and then dropped the paper in its little lead case into the well.

On hearing this the victim would hasten to the well to pay for its removal. If the sum offered was considered enough (it cost more to remove a curse than to put one in) psalms would be recited, a passage from the Scriptures read, the little lead case would be pulled up and the well-keeper would pronounce the curse lifted.

Saint Elian's Well exists only in name now, for the water has been drained away. No one regrets this, except perhaps the well-keepers.

THE DEVIL'S BRIDGE

THE Devil's Bridge is one of the beauty spots of Wales. Holidaymakers from all over the world come to visit it. They walk across the bridge, they look down on the roaring, turbulent waters below, and pass on. Few of them stop to ask how it got its name, or pause to wonder what the Devil was doing building bridges in this peaceful and lovely corner of Cardiganshire.

Now it came about in this wise. An old woman once lived here called Megan of Llandunach and she was in sore trouble because her one and only cow had wandered, she knew not how, over to the other side of the deep ravine down which the River Mynach rushed and swirled and hissed and bubbled like the magic brew in a witches' cauldron.

As she stood there weeping and wringing her hands, a voice behind her said, 'What is the matter, Megan?', and turning round she saw a man, cowled like a monk, a rosary in his hand; and because she was so distracted she told him all her troubles. 'Do not worry,' said the monk, 'I will build you a bridge and all will be well.' 'But Sir,' cried Megan, 'I am poor, I could never repay you.' 'I want no pay', answered the monk. 'Give me but the first living creature that crosses the bridge and I will be satisfied. Now go back to your cottage and when all is finished I will call you.'

But the old woman was not so foolish as she seemed. She noticed something strange about the foot of this obliging stranger and his knees too, surely they were behind instead of in front. So when she heard the monk calling her she took with her a loaf of bread and her little black dog.

'There is a fine bridge for you,' said the stranger proudly, and sure enough, there it was stretching from side to side of the yawning chasm. 'Yes,' said the old woman, 'it is a bridge sure enough, but is it strong?' 'Strong?' said the builder, indignantly. 'Of course it is strong.'

'Will it bear the weight of this loaf?' asked Megan. The monk laughed scornfully. 'Try it and see', he said. So Megan bent down and rolled the loaf over the bridge, and the little black dog bounded after it, snapping at it with its little white teeth. 'It is indeed a good bridge', she said; 'Thank you, kind sir. My little dog was the first to cross it and now he is yours.'

'Keep your silly dog, he is no use to me,' roared the monk, stamping his foot in fury; and then suddenly he was gone.

Only a smell of brimstone remained to tell Megan that she had indeed outwitted the Devil. But she and the cow and the little dog lived happily ever after. And this is how the Bad Man's bridge was built.

ST. BEUNO AND THE CURLEW

WHEN we hear the haunting cry of the curlew on the Welsh hills, we know that the Spring has come. Egg collectors go out to try and find its nest, but few of them succeed, for the curlew's eggs are harder to find than rubies and this is how it came about.

When St. Beuno lived at Clynnog, he used to preach at Llanddwyn, walking on the sea with his book of sermons which he always carried with him. One day he dropped this precious book into the water and it was swept away by the tide. The Saint was much troubled for sermons are not easy to write, even for a Saint. Imagine then his joy when he found his book laid safely on a stone, with a curlew mounting guard over it.

Kneeling down on the sea-shore, the Saint prayed that God would send a blessing on the curlew as a reward for this good deed, and ever since then Nature has given protection to these long-billed birds, so that those who seek to take their eggs will seldom find them.

TWM SHÔN CATTI

A GAY highwayman who robbed the rich to give to the poor was Twm Shôn Catti, the Welsh Robin Hood. His cave near the source of the Towy can be seen to this day. Many and varied were the adventures he had, and the tricks he played.

One day, riding a weary old horse with a load of sea-shells in his saddle-bag, he met another highwayman whom he knew to be wicked and cruel. Twm pretended to be frightened and cowered back begging for mercy, as the rogue demanded his money or his life. Then at pistol point he loosed his saddle-bags and before he could be stopped, heaved them over the hedge.

Cursing him, the highwayman scrambled through the thorns after them. As his opponent bent to pick up the saddle-bags, Twm left his weary old hack and sprang on to the saddle of the highwayman's beautiful mare. 'Go like the wind, my lovely,' he urged, and they galloped away out of sight in the twinkling of an eye.

Outwitted and cursing, with the sea-shells scattered at his feet, the highwayman saw even the old horse canter slowly out of sight before he could regain the road. Away over the hill Twm was examining the well-filled saddle-bags on his new horse with many a chuckle.

THE WHITE COW OF MITCHELL'S FOLD

NEAR Corndon Hill on the Welsh borderland stands an ancient stone circle known as Mitchell's Fold.

Years ago, so the story goes, there was a grievous famine in the land and many folk would have starved to death if it had not been for a beautiful little white fairy cow that stood on this spot night and morning and gave milk to all who came and asked for it.

Every day the long procession of people would wind up the hill path with their pails and basins and pitchers. It mattered not what vessels they took; as long as they only took one apiece there was plenty for all.

One day there came an old witch called Mitchell, a bad old woman she was with a spite against everyone. The neighbours wondered what she carried under her long red cloak as she followed them up the hill, but she showed no one what it was and no one dared ask her. Only after they had all gone home did she bring out a sieve, and she milked and milked and milked until there was no milk left, and from that day the fairy cow disappeared and was never seen again.

But the old witch got her punishment, for she was turned into one of the stones on the hill-side and all the other stones were put round her to keep her in. And there, with the winds blowing over them and the curlews crying above them, they stand to this day.

THE ROARING BULL OF BAGBURY

AT Bagbury Farm, near Hyssington, there once lived a wicked farmer, so fierce-tempered and vicious, so free with his knocks and kicks, that the whole parish went in fear of him. But one day he met his match for he kicked an old witch, and she, turning on him, uttered this curse: 'As you are wicked in life, so shall you be in death. Your soul shall never rest.'

84

Soon after this the bad man died, and, in the form of a bull, his ghost roamed the country-side, striking terror into every heart and doing more damage than a dozen wicked farmers. The men dared not go out to till the fields, the women feared to hang out their washing, and the children stayed from school afraid to venture beyond the door. At nights the bull would go roaring up and down, shaking the cottage walls, bringing down tiles and shutters and breaking the crockery and furniture. At last, in despair, the villagers went to the parson and begged him to come with Bell, Book, and Candle and lay the bull. The parson said that if they could persuade the bull to go into the church he would come, and twelve other parsons with him. So all the people stole out of their houses, and, creeping for protection along the walls and hedges, they got closer and closer to the bull, while the parson read texts to him to keep him quiet. And between them they got the bull into the church, and all the people crowded in too, and they bolted and barred the door. Then the bell tolled, and the parsons stood up with their books and candles and began to read, and as they read the bull seemed to grow quieter and smaller, and they thought they had got him. Suddenly he gave a mighty roar, and blew out all the candles. The readers faltered and stopped. For a moment there was silence. Then in the darkness the bull began to swell again and he swelled to such a size that he cracked the walls of the church, and all was wild confusion. But one old blind parson, more cunning than the rest, had hidden his lighted candle in his top-boot, and when the darkness came he shouted: 'Light your candles from mine!' This they did, and so the reading went on, till at last the bull grew so small that they were able to push him into a boot which one of the congregation lent for the purpose, and they laced it securely and tied it so tightly that nothing could undo it. Then they buried him under the doorstep of the church, and no man dare move the stone, for it is said:

If ever man shall raise this stone
In Hyssington once more this bull shall roam.

The Enchanted Pool

Silent the Pool lies under the dark sky.
A wind comes from the sea,
hovers with folded wing upon the margin;
then turning in a breath,
with dragging tread as one that moves in a nightmare,
returns soft-footed over the soundless dunes.
A stealthy moon appears,
only to draw in closer folds
the heavy sombre curtains of the sky.
The Pool is alone,
save for a wakened dreamer, and a bird
that frets and frets and wonders that it sleeps no
more. . . .

These hear as from unutterable depths
a muffled voice that calls
to listeners they see not:
murmuring soft words as if to lovers,
and words of praise as if to beautiful women,
and fiercer words of war as if to soldiers. . . .

And bird and dreamer suddenly
feel how the blinded night grows tangible,
and shudder in their solitary vigil
to hear through the thick dark
a buried city calling to its ghosts. . . .

MELFIN JONES

ARTHUR & HIS SLEEPING WARRIORS

ONCE upon a time a young Welsh drover came to London driving his herd of Black Welsh cattle. He carried a stout hazel stick as drovers always do, and having sold his cattle with much profit, he came to London Bridge to gaze with wonder and awe on the shops and people so strange to his country-bred eyes.

Suddenly a man stopped and began to talk to him, asking him whence he came, and the Welshman answered him surlily, for he did not like being questioned by strangers. 'Do you remember where you got that stick?' asked the man. 'That has nothing to do with you,' answered the drover. 'Ah, but I think it has,' said the stranger, 'for there is treasure hidden near that spot. Lead me to it and you will have great riches.'

Then the drover knew that he was talking to a sorcerer and he was afraid. But the desire for riches was stronger than fear, and they set out together for the land of Wales.

When they got to Craig y Dinas, the Rock of the Fortress at the head of the Neath Valley, the Welshman stopped. 'This is where I cut my stick,' he said. The sorcerer knelt down and began to dig; soon he uncovered a large flat stone. Prising this up they found steps leading downwards and at the bottom there was a door. 'Will you come?' said the sorcerer. 'I will,' replied the Welshman, for now his curiosity was indeed greater than his fear. Inside the door hung a mighty bell. 'Do not touch it,' whispered the sorcerer, 'or it will be the end of both of us.'

They went on into a vast lofty cave, and here a strange sight met their eyes. In the centre was a great round table; seated at the table and stretched on the floor were thousands of soldiers clad in armour, their shields on their arms and their spears by their side. They were all fast asleep. On a golden throne sat a King of gigantic stature, a gold crown on his head, and in his hand a mighty sword. He too, was sunk in slumber.

'Who are they?' whispered the drover.

'They are Arthur's warriors,' answered the sorcerer. 'Those at the table are his Knights and Arthur himself sits on the throne with his sword Excalibur in his hand. They have slept here for a thousand years waiting for the time when Wales will need them once more on the throne at Caer Lleon.'

'What will awaken them?' asked the drover.

'Only the great bell that hangs at the entrance to the cave,' said the sorcerer. 'Now come, we must be quick.'

On the floor of the cave were piles of gold and they filled their bags, and hurried back to the entrance.

'How I would like to see them all awakening,' thought the drover; 'I will just touch the bell as I pass and see what happens.' Never had he heard such a noise; it clanged and echoed round and round the stone vaulting of the caves, and mingled with it was the clanking of armour as the warriors rose to their feet and snatched up their weapons. Then came a deep voice saying, 'Who rang the bell? Has the day come?'

'No, no,' cried the sorcerer, shaking like an aspen leaf, 'the day has not come, sleep on.' Again the voice spoke, 'The bell has rung. Awake, Arthur the Great.'

'No,' screamed the sorcerer, 'it is still night, sleep on.' Then Arthur rose to his feet, the jewels in his crown shining like bright stars. His voice was clear and sweet like running water as he said 'The day has not yet come. Sleep on, my warriors, the morn of Wales has not yet dawned.'

Slowly the great company sank once more into a deep sleep and all was silent.

Terror-striken the drover turned and fled out into the sunlight. When he looked, round the sorcerer had disappeared, so had the cave, and though he searched every inch of the ground he never found the entrance again.

86

THE DRUMS OF CWM

HEARD from across the valley it is a strange uncanny sound. The night is calm and still but from the hill-side, with its wooded cwms, comes a deep booming roar. Is it the wind, or is it really the drums beaten by a dead man's hand, the ghost of the Drummer who, beating The Retreat to the end, was slain with all his comrades and lies buried with his drums on this wild hill-side in Montgomeryshire?

It is said that when these drums are heard disaster will follow, and it is true to this day that the 'Roaring of the Cwms' heralds the approaching storm.

OFFA'S DYKE

THE borderland of Wales was often the scene of strife in early days. Offa, King of Mercia (A.D. 757–96), built a dyke as boundary between his kingdom and Wales, extending from near Bristol northwards to near Prestatyn, a distance of about 100 miles. The dyke may be followed to this day.

Tradition says that when a Welshman crossed Offa's Dyke, a limb if not his life was forfeit, and the reprisals of the Welsh were equally vigorous. The long dyke has carried its malignant name down through history.

The New Sword of Song

Behold a nation here in miniature—
The van of thought and rear of humble toil:
Those who command, and those who must endure,
Linked by a common love of native soil.
Here in the eyes of age and youth converge
The mystic fires oppression may not veil—
Red flaming zeal that made Glyndŵr a scourge;
White breathless visions of a distant Grail. . . .

O for a harp that might translate in song
These dumb desires, this strength that will not bend;
And soaring find the Light men sought so long
Through blind mistaken roads that knew no end:
Singing to nations paralysed with fear,
'Seek not a sword—Excalibur is here!'

MELFIN JONES

THE WOMEN OF STRUMBLE HEAD

STRUMBLE HEAD   M. Wight

WHEN the sea dashes against the rocks of Strumble Head, it is rarely remembered that an episode in the history of our island was played on this wild headland of Wales.

A French fleet, determined to force a landing somewhere on the British coast, was sighted, as it sailed past St. David's Head on 22 February 1797. Fourteen hundred Frenchmen landed that day but they surrendered unconditionally, overcome by surprise and fear at the appearance of what seemed a formidable army assembling against them. The same shock caused the French fleet to up-anchor and away, abandoning the invasion when they saw an ever-growing defending force which would cause a battle the size of which they had never dreamed.

Lord Cawdor had indeed rallied 'an army!' Round and round the headland and on the distant hills there marched and counter-marched the women of Pembrokeshire, armed with mattocks, spades, scythes, and reaping-hooks, clad in their red cloaks and tall beaver hats; while in the foreground, the Castle Martin Yeomanry galloping about were mistaken for the staff officers of a large and imposing army. In Fishguard Church is a monument to 'Jemima Nicholas, a tall, stout, masculine female, who worked as a shoe-maker and a cobbler, who took a pitchfork and boldly marched to Pen Cae to meet the foe'. Jemima captured twelve Frenchmen and marched them off to the guard-house in Fishguard. The Siôl Jemima or Red Shawl is named after her.

So it was that some Welsh women routed the French in a bloodless skirmish, to become for ever after known as The Women of Strumble Head.

THE BATTLE OF CROGEN

NEAR Chirk Castle, where Offa's Dyke sweeps down into the Ceiriog Valley, can be seen the gap in the dyke which was made to enable merchants to pass. This was the scene of the famous battle of Crogen, during the third expedition of Henry II of England to subjugate the Welsh. Henry, having failed twice before in this object, collected an enormous army of troops from all his dominions, England, Normandy, Flanders, Anjou, and Guienne. They encamped at Oswestry. Against him came Owain Gwynedd and Cadwaladr, sons of Gruffydd, and the whole forces of Gwynedd, Lord Rhys and the forces of south Wales, Owain Cyfeiliog, Madog ap Maredudd with the men of Powys, and many others.

These gathered at Corwen, a strong position defended by the Berwyn mountains. When the Welsh would not advance out of the mountainous country which would give them some advantage over their more numerous foes, Henry became impatient and marched forward up the Ceiriog Valley, preceded by vast numbers of woodcutters to clear the forest before him. They reached the gap in Offa's Dyke at the place called Crogen; 'And there a few Welshmen came bravely to oppose him.' So many were slain that the place is called 'Adwy'r Beddau, or the Pass of the Graves, to this day, and for many years the English used the word Crogen to denote a warrior of desperate courage.

Despite this setback, Henry led his army to the Berwyn Hills, but there the elements completed the work of that gallant little Welsh band. There fell such rain that 'the King's men could scant stand upon their feet upon these slipperie hilles', and Henry was forced to withdraw his army with great loss of both men and materials without accomplishing his purpose.

He is reported later to have informed the Emperor Emanuel of Constantinople that 'in a certain part of the island there was a people, called Welsh, so bold and ferocious that when unarmed they did not fear to encounter an armed force, being ready to shed their blood in defence of their country, and to sacrifice their lives for renown, which is the more surprising, as the beasts of the field over the whole face of the island became gentle, but these desperate men could not be tamed'.

(Quotations from Giraldus's *Description of Wales*.)

The Farewell of Owain Glyndŵr

Draw near, my friends, . . . One thing must yet be told,
Ere steeped in silent death the teller lies.
You that have loved a warrior spent and old,
'Tis you alone shall witness where he dies. . . .

Once, when the morning glimmered chill and grey
By Valle Crucis walls, but strangely soared
To sudden fire, I chanced to go that way
And saw the aged Abbot walk abroad.
Then, as in jocund mood I passed him by
And jested that he rose so long ere noon,
He capped the jest—'Tis thou, Glyndŵr, not I,
That walk'st too soon—a hundred years too soon.'

. . . And in my prime I scorned the words he said;
But now, in dying, live again that dawn,
And grieve that of a truth my land has bled
In travail for the dreams of Time unborn. . . .

Last night a falling star passed over me;
Perchance my star, that blazed and burnt away,
For in the heavens it wrote my destiny—
Woe to the dreamer born before his day. . . .
Now, friends, I take my dreams and lay them still,
Even with this weary sword at rest from war.
Give me some hollow in a quiet hill
Where I may sleep in peace but dream no more.

MELFIN JONES

89

Up in the mountains is the drovers' track,
The path our fathers made long ages back,
How small is man, his thoughts, his pride, his fears,
How strong the hills of God
Stand steadfast through the years;
And as the mist breaks in the evening light,
A shepherd with his sheep moves slowly into sight.
Thus through the passing years,
Though man so often fails,
This parable lives on among the hills of Wales.

HETHER KAY

WELSH MUSIC

NATIONAL FOLK-SONGS

Wele Gwawriodd: Lo! A Day Dawned

Bugeilio'r Gwenith Gwyn: Watching the Wheat

Suo-Gân: Lullaby

Robin Goch: Robin Redbreast

Dechreuad y Byd: The Beginning of the World

Ar Hyd y Nos: All Through the Night

Dafydd y Garreg Wen: David of the White Rock

Cyfri'r Geifr: Counting the Goats

LLANWDDYN JIG

Croen y Ddafad Felan: The Yellow Sheepskin

WELE GWAWRIODD

Geiriau gan
HENRY WILLIAMS, BETHESDA
(Alaw Llechid) *c.* 1849

*CAINC WERIN

1. We - le gwawriodd dydd i'w
2. Duw a'n cof - iodd, Duw a'n
3. Ha - le - liw - ia, Ha - le -

gof - io, Ge - ni Sei - lo go - raf swydd; We - le
ca - rodd, Duw o - so - dodd Ie - su'n Iawn; Duw er
-liw - ia! Aeth i'r lladd - fa yn ein lle; Ha - le -

*Trwy ganiatad Cymdeithas Alawon Gwerin Cymru

ddyn - ion mwy na modd - ion, Ddônt â rhodd - ion i ddo'n rhwydd. Hen a-
syn - dod ddar - fu gan - fod Trefn goll'-yng - dod i ni'n llawn. Duw ry-
-liw - ia, Ha - le - liw - ia! Duw sy'n fod - lon yn - ddo Fe. Sain "Ho-

-dde - wid E - den od - iaeth, We - le he - ddiw ddaeth i ben; We - le
-fe - ddir, I - ddo ce - nir Gan dri - gol - ion nef a llawr, Tra bydd
-san - na i Fab Da - fydd" Ie - su beu - nydd fy - ddo'n ben; Am ei

drefn - iad dwy - fol gar - iad, O flaen ein lly - gaid heb un llen.
Ie - su, fu mewn gwae - ledd, 'N eistedd ar yr or - sedd fawr.
haedd - iant sy'n o - gon - iant, By - dded mol - iant mwy, A - men.

Trefn. D. E.

93

BUGEILIO'R GWENITH GWYN

WIL HOPCYN
Tr. WIL IFAN

ALAW WERIN

1 Mi sydd fachgen ifanc ffôl.
   Yn byw yn ôl fy ffansi
   Myfi'n bugeilio'r gwenith gwyn,
   Ac arall yn ei fedi.
   Pam na ddeui ar fy ôl,
   Ryw ddydd ar ôl ei gilydd?
   Gwaith 'rwy'n dy weld, y feinir fach,
   Yn lanach, lanach beunydd!

2 Glanach, glanach wyt bob dydd,
   Neu fi sy â'm ffydd yn ffolach,
   Er mwyn y gŵr a wnaeth dy wedd,
   Gwna im drugaredd bellach.
   Cwn dy ben, gwêl acw draw.
   Rho i mi'th law, Wen dirion;
   Gwaith yn dy fynwes bert ei thro
   Mae allwedd clo fy nghalon!

1 A foolish luckless youth am I,
   Love's sweet commandments keeping;
   'Tis I who watch the golden wheat,
   Another does the reaping.
   Come, oh, come when true love calls;
   Than all the flowers thou'rt rarer,
   My love but grows as thy fond charms
   Grow fairer yet and fairer.

2 Fairer and yet fairer blooms
   My wistful eyes discover;
   For His dear sake, who fashioned thee,
   Show mercy to thy lover.
   Oh, lift thine eyes on my despair,
   Lead me to Heaven's portal.
   For on thy girdle are the keys
   To ev'ry joy immortal.

94

SUO-GÂN

ROBERT BRYAN
English words by HETHER KAY

ALAW WERIN

1 Huna blentyn ar fy mynwes,
Clyd a chynnes ydyw hon;
Breichiau mam sy'n dynn amdanat
Cariad mam sy dan fy mron.
Ni chaiff dim amharu'th gyntun.
Ni wna undyn â thi gam;
Huna'n dawel annwyl blentyn,
Huna'n fwyn ar fron dy fam.

2 Huna'n dawel heno, huna,
Huna'n fwyn y tlws ei lun;
Pam yr wyt yn awr yn gwenu,
Gwenu'n dirion yn dy hun?
Ai angylion fry sy'n gwenu
Arnat ti yn gwenu'n llon?
Tithau'n gwenu'n ôl dy huno,
Huna'n dawel ar fy mron.

1 Sleep my baby, night has fallen,
Cuddle closely safe and warm;
Angels wakeful, watching o'er you,
Guard my darling till the dawn.
Sweet, there's nothing here can hurt you,
Stars are twinkling, moonbeams play;
Sleep my baby, sleep and fear not
Till the breaking of the day.

2 Softly night-time now shall bless you
With its stillness calm and deep;
Little baby, are you smiling
As you gently fall asleep?
Far above the heavenly angels
Smiling too with you so blessed;
Joyous they look down upon you,
Calmly sleeping and at rest.

95

ROBIN GOCH

Welsh words, first verse traditional,
the remaining verses, and the English words
by LLEW TEGID

Welsh Folk Song arranged by
J. LLOYD WILLIAMS

Moderato

Ro - bin Goch ar ben y rhin - iog, A'i ddwy a - den fach an
Wel-come Rob - in with thy greet - ing, On the thresh - old meek-ly

wyd - og; Ac yn dwe - dyd yn ys - ma - la "Mae hi'n
wait - ing, To the chil - dren's home now en - ter, From the

oer mi ddaw yn ei - ra, Mae hi'n oer mi ddaw yn ei - ra."
cold and snow of win - ter, From the cold and snow of win - ter.

By permission of Hughes and Son, 16 Westgate Street, Cardiff.

96

3 Robin Goch a'i goesau meinion,
　Yn y rhew a'i draed yn oerion,
　Dwêd ei gŵyn bob hwyr a borau,
　'Mae y rhew yn brathu 'modiau'.

4 Robin tyrd a dwêd dy hanes,
　Ni ddaw rhew i galon gynnes,
　Tyrd i'r cwmni ac ymdwyma,
　'Mae hi'n oer mi ddaw yn eira'.

5 Robin Goch mor fwyn dy drydar,
　Wyt ffyddlonaf o'r holl adar,
　Mae y gaeaf oer yn gwgu,
　Ti gei loches ymai lechu.

3 Come in Robin, do not fear us,
　Thy bright eye and chirping cheer us;
　Thy sad note excite our pity,
　Now the frost begins to bite thee.

4 Robin come and tell thy story,
　Leave outside thy care and worry;
　Tell the children, Robin dearest,
　Of the babies in the forest.

5 Of the flame that burnt thy bosom,
　Of thy wand'rings far and lonesome,
　Of thy home among the greenwood,
　Of thy happy days of childhood.

DECHREUAD Y BYD

HEN ALAW

By permission of Undeb Cymanfaoedd Canu Alawon Cenedlaethol Cymru.

1 Daeth min yr hwyr a'i hyfryd hedd
  Ar fro sy'n dawel fel y bedd;
  Mae'r adar mân a'u hodlau mwyn
  Yn awr yn fud yng nghôl y llwyn.
  Yn plygu'i ben mae'r rhosyn teg.
  A cheir i'w suo chwaon chweg;
  I'w gartre'r gŵr gyfeiria'i gam,
  A'r baban gwsg ar fron ei fam.

2 O! orig hoff ym mrig yr hwyr,
  Tangnefedd biau 'nghôl yn llwyr;
  Yng nghwmni myfyrdodau fyrdd,
  Ymlwybro wnaf hyd wlithog ffyrdd;
  Teimladau dwys fy nghalon lawn,
  Ni ddichon iaith eu traethu'n iawn;
  A'm dymuniadau'm min yr hwyr,
  Nid oes ond Duw ei hun a'u gŵyr.

99

AR HYD Y NOS

ARRANGED FOR S.A. WITH PIANO ACCOMPANIMENT

The Words by CEIRIOG

Arranged by W. REES LEWIS

Holl amrantau'r sêr ddywedant,
    Ar hyd y nos,—
'Dyma'r ffordd i fro gogoniant,'
    Ar hyd y nos.
Golau arall yw tywyllwch,
I arddangos gwir brydferthwch
Teulu'r nefoedd mewn tawelwch,
    Ar hyd y nos.

O, mor siriol gwena'r seren
    Ar hyd y nos,
I oleuo'i chwaer ddaearen
    Ar hyd y nos.
Nos yw henaint pan ddaw cystudd,
Ond i harddu dyn a'i hwyr ddyd,
Rhown ein golau gwan i'n gilydd,
    Ar hyd y nos.

Deep the silence round us spreading,
    All through the night.
Dark the path that we are treading,
    All through the night.
Still the coming day discerning
By the hope within us burning
To the dawn our footsteps turning,
    All through the night.

Star of faith the dark adorning—
    All through the night,
Lead us fearless towards the morning,
    All through the night.
Though our hearts be wrapped in sorrow
From the hope of dawn we borrow
Promise of a glad to-morrow—
    All through the night.

DAFYDD Y GARREG WEN

Words by CEIRIOG
Tr. A. L. SALMON

Trefn. W. D.

CYFRI'R GEIFR

Geiriau traddodiadol

Tr. D. E. PARRY WILLIAMS

Cymedrol

Yn gyflymach

*Newidier y lliw o bennill i bennill, c.e., *las, goch, binc, ddu; finlas, gynffonlas*, etc.

104

LLANWDDYN JIG

THIS dance was seen by members of the Girl Guide Association and was noted in 1950 by Betty Michael, Training Adviser for Wales, from the dancing of a shepherd in the Berwyn Hills between Bala and Vyrnwy. He claimed to know four dances, handed down to him from his father and grandfather; but all were of the same name, *Croen y ddafad felan*, which is the name of a tune widely associated with this kind of dance in north Wales. This particular version is performed in ordinary shoes by one man; or sometimes by two in competition. In other districts, not far away, similar dances are performed in clogs. The shepherd accompanied himself on a mouth-organ.

Two split sticks are laid on the ground; a long one, in the line of the dance, and a short one across. The first dance or variation is performed in the angles on each side of the long stick. The second is performed with a cross step over the long stick up to the centre and back. In the third, the hands are clapped over and under each leg in turn; and in the fourth, a lighted candle in a bottle takes the place of the crossed sticks. Another variation is the passing of a broom handle from hand to hand under each leg in turn.

There are several step-sequences, and the proficiency of the dancer is assessed by the number of different steps he can perform. The right heel is generally brought down smartly for the start, and the dance finished with a stamp, L. R. L. RR.

(*a*) Toe and heel and heel toe.

Left:			t h	T			h	T			t h	T		t h	T			
Right:	h	T			t h	T			h		t h	T				h	&c.	

(*b*) Single change heel tap.

Left:			h T		h T		h T		h T		h T		
Right:	h	T	h	T	h	T	h	T	h	T	h	&c.	

(*c*) Cross step, starting with one foot each side of stick.

Left of stick:				Tr Hr			Tr Hr		
Right of stick:		Tl Hl				Tl Hl			&c.

The letters t and h represent toe and heel taps. H represents a hop, on left, l, or on right, r. T represents the supporting foot, lowered to the ball to take the weight of the body.

THE DANCE

Bars of music

I

Standing with feet close together on each side of the long stick, near the angles.

8   Step (*a*) tapping alternate heels in opposite angle.

8   Step (*b*) tapping alternate heels in opposite angle.

II

8   Step (*a*) in left angle.

8   Step (*c*) cross step over the long stick up to centre and back.

III

8   Step (*a*) in position as in I.

8   Double hop on each foot in turn, clapping hands under and over the raised leg.

IV

With lighted candle instead of sticks.

8   Step (*a*) tapping the heel to the side, instead of across.

8   Double hop on each foot, swinging the free leg over the candle; swinging the right foot first.

105

With a besom, instead of crossed sticks.

8   Step (*a*) as in IV.

8   Double hop step passing the broom-handle from one hand to the other under the free leg.

These variations may be taken as many times as desired; either separately or in sequence.

CROEN Y DDAFAD FELAN

Arr. J. MEGAN WILLIAMS

FIRST PRINTED AT THE UNIVERSITY PRESS, OXFORD
THIS EDITION REPRINTED LITHOGRAPHICALLY BY CSP PRINTING OF CARDIFF